30 WAYS TO DIVORCE-PROOF YOUR MARRIAGE

30 WAYS TO
DIVORCE
PROOF
YOUR MARRIAGE

Practical and Proven Strategies for
a Lasting and Joyful Union

Julius and Mary Eniolu

www.eternalharmonyretreats.com

30 Ways to Divorce-Proof Your Marriage
Practical and Proven Strategies for a Lasting and Joyful Union
Copyright © Julius and Mary Eniolu 2025
www.eternalharmonyretreats.com

The right of Julius and Mary Eniolu to be identified as the Authors
of this work has been asserted by them in accordance with the
Copyright, Designs and Patents Act 1988

All Scripture quotations unless otherwise stated are taken from the
Holy
Bible, New International Version (NIV) copyright © 1973, 1978,
1984, 2011 by the International Bible Society. Used by permission

First printed May 2025

Layout and Design by Manoj Gupta

Printed in England

A CIP catalogue record for this title is available from the British
Library

ISBN 978-0-9957861-1-0

Published by Can Do Ventures Limited, England, United Kingdom

DEDICATION

To every couple longing to experience true oneness in their union, and to every single person with a vision to build a strong, healthy marriage and family—This book is for you. May it serve as a compass, guiding you with wisdom, encouragement, and hope toward a relationship far greater than you ever imagined.

And to our three incredible sons—You are living proof that love, faith, and intentionality can build something truly beautiful. May you carry this legacy forward with strength, grace and wisdom. Happy reading.

ACKNOWLEDGEMENT

We want to say heartfelt thanks to our parents. Thank you for laying the foundation for the values we live by today and for the people we have become. Your love, faith, and steadfast commitment to your marriages taught us what it means to show up—for each other, for your families, and for God. You didn't just talk about values; you lived them in front of us.

Your lives have been a constant reminder that love is a choice—one that must be made daily. You showed us that marriage isn't always easy, but with faith, grace, dedication, a commitment to walking in the same direction, and with God at the centre, a marriage can thrive through every season.

We stand on your shoulders with deep gratitude, knowing that much of who we are—both as individuals and as a couple—was shaped by your quiet strength and enduring love. Thank you for the legacy you've passed down. We carry it with us every day—and now, we pass it on.

We are deeply grateful to Dr. Albert Oduwole, CEO of MarryMatics Consult Ltd, for graciously taking the time to read through our manuscript and for honouring us by writing the forward to this book. Your thoughtful words, encouragement, and endorsement mean so much to us. Thank you for believing in the message of this book and for lending your voice to its mission.

Last and certainly not least, we would like to say thank you to the Almighty God, our heavenly Father, for giving us your enduring Word that has been our compass on this journey helping us navigate the storms of life with grace and strength. We could not have come this far without you.

CONTENTS

FORWARD

We Get Better with Repetition—Except in Marriage

We tend to get better at making choices the more we make them. That's true when it comes to buying cars, houses, gadgets, and just about everything else in life—except marriage. With marriage, you must make your best choice the *first* time. There's no room for rehearsals, and mistakes can be costly and painful.

Laugh and Learn

A computer typist was instructed to type *"1 John 4:18"* on the front cover of a wedding booklet. Unfortunately, he accidentally typed *"John 4:18"* instead.

Here's the difference:

> 1 John 4:18: *"There is no fear in love. But perfect love drives out fear, because fear has to do with punishment. The one who fears is not made perfect in love"*

> John 4:18: *"The fact is, you have had five husbands, and the man you now have is not your husband..."*

Can you imagine the embarrassment that little mistake caused, especially for the bride? Just the absence of a single '1' made all the difference.

No Institution

There's no institution where marriage is formally taught, yet marriage is the only institution where you get the certificate before you begin the learning. *(Selah)* So how do you avoid making a mistake that could last a lifetime? The answer is *mentoring.* I define mentoring as gaining the benefit of someone else's experience—getting the *learning* without paying the *tuition.* In this way, mentoring surpasses experience as the best teacher.

That's why you're holding in your hands one of the most dynamic mentoring tools for choosing the right partner and divorce-proofing your marriage: a book written by Julius and Mary Eniolu, a couple with over 30 years of marital experience.

With sound scriptural foundation and practical insight, they've done an exceptional job showing you how to *enjoy,* not just *endure,* your marriage.

So let me get out of your way, so you can READ, RUMINATE, and RECOMMEND this book.

Dr. Albert Oduwole
International Conference Speaker
CEO, MarryMatics Consult Ltd.

INTRODUCTION

A healthy, happy, and lasting marriage isn't a fairytale—it's entirely possible. But it doesn't happen by chance. It takes intentionality, consistent effort, and a shared vision.

After 30 years of marriage—as at the time of writing this book—we've learned that building a fulfilling relationship is both a journey and a daily decision, and the principles we share in this book is what has helped us build a home filled with joy, laughter, growth, and peace.

This book isn't a collection of theories or abstract advice. It's a heartfelt offering of real-life insights, timeless principles, and practical takeaways drawn from our lived experience as husband and wife. Rooted in faith and strengthened by daily commitment, it reflects the lessons we've learned—sometimes the hard way—about what it truly takes to thrive as a couple.

Inside, you'll find down-to-earth guidance and actionable steps designed to help you deepen your connection, improve communication, and navigate the inevitable ups and downs of marriage. You'll also find an emphasis on personal growth—because strong relationships begin with strong individuals.

We believe that when two people intentionally invest in their relationship, they can build something extraordinary—not just for themselves, but for generations to come. The insights and guidance shared in this book can empower *any* couple *willing* to invest in their relationship, to build a strong relationship and leave an amazing legacy.

So come along with us on this journey, as we share our life and story with you. Our hope is that you'll discover inspiration, encouragement, and practical wisdom to create the vibrant, joyful, and resilient marriage you've always desired—one intentional step at a time.

1

BEFORE YOU SAY "I DO"

Laying the Right Foundation:
Choosing the Right Partner

The most crucial part of any building is its foundation. It determines whether the structure will be weak or strong, and the taller the building, the deeper and stronger the foundation must be. Marriage is no different. If we desire a union that can withstand the inevitable pressures of life—financial strain, parenting challenges, loss, unemployment, illness, and more—the foundation must be solid. And that foundation begins with choosing the right partner. So, if you are reading this book and are not yet married, you have a great opportunity to get it right from the start.

Many marriages are set up for failure from the very beginning simply because the parties involved did not make a wise choice in selecting their life partner. One of the key reasons we have remained steadfast in our marriage, even during the most challenging seasons, is our unwavering conviction that we made the right choice when we chose each other, and that our union is God's will.

We are confident that we were meant to be together. So, when trials arise—and we have faced many—we do not question whether we made a mistake. Doubt is a dangerous seed. When you start questioning if you married the right person, it's only a matter of time before you convince yourself that you didn't. If difficulties persist, that seed of doubt can grow into full-blown regret, eventually leading to the belief that the only way forward is to undo the supposed mistake. This is how many go from saying "I do" to declaring "I'm done."

You may be wondering: how can one be certain—out of the billions of people in the world—that they have chosen the right person? As Christians, the Bible is our foundation, and its truths and principles serve as our guide. Our faith shapes our beliefs, influences our decisions, and determines how we live. When it came to choosing a spouse, we did not rely solely on emotions or fleeting feelings; we allowed God to lead us. Through prayer and divine guidance, we both came to the conviction that we were meant for each other. God can and will lead you too—if you ask Him.

Common Mistakes in Choosing a Life Partner

Many people make emotional, impulsive, or culturally influenced decisions when choosing a spouse, leading to heartbreak and disappointment. Let's examine some of the most common mistakes:

Prioritizing Looks Over Character

Many people base their choice of a partner primarily on physical appearance. When asked about their ideal spouse, they often describe external features—a tall, handsome man with a muscular build, or a slim, long-haired woman. Social media and cultural influences have exacerbated unrealistic expectations, leading people to seek an idealized version of a partner rather than someone with depth and substance.

The reality is that physical appearance changes over time. Beauty fades, muscles weaken, and the six-pack may turn into a one-pack with a dot in the middle! A marriage built on physical attraction alone is bound to crumble, and prioritizing looks and chemistry over shared values, common interests, and, most importantly, character is really a recipe for disaster in future.

Ignoring Red Flags and Hoping for Change

Another mistake commonly made, is ignoring glaring warning signs in the early stages of a relationship, convincing yourself that things will improve over time. It could be tempting to dismiss dishonesty, lack of emotional control, irresponsibility, or controlling behaviours because you are "in love." However, these red flags do not disappear— they only become more pronounced as the relationship progresses and the initial excitement wanes. If before marriage, something about your partner deeply concerns you, do not ignore it! It is far easier to walk away before marriage than to spend years in a painful and unhealthy relationship, hoping for change that may never come.

Entering a Relationship with the Intention of Changing the Other Person

One of the biggest traps in marriage is believing that you can change your spouse. The truth is you cannot change anyone—only God can transform hearts. If there are traits or behaviours in your partner that you struggle with now, they will not magically disappear after marriage.

Early in our marriage, we both made the mistake of trying to change each other. It led only to frustration and disappointment. Ever found yourself asking this question of your spouse "why can't you be more like me?" perhaps not verbally, but in your heart? If we are to be honest, we've all been there and done that, but the reality is, they are not meant to be like you.

In our marriage, we often joke that Julius is the "public relations officer" of the family—a natural people person with a gift for smoothing things over and building connections. The downside?

That same gift can have him chatting on the phone for an hour, completely oblivious to the fact that we're already running late for an appointment!

Mary, on the other hand, is the strategist—the one who maps out the plan, keeps everyone on track, and ensures goals are met (case in point: this book! 😊). Of course, her strength has its own quirks too—sometimes, being so laser focussed on getting things done can make her come across as a bit overbearing.

Over the years, we have learned an important truth: our differences were not meant to divide us but to complement us and every day, we are learning to appreciate and celebrate each other's strengths because we both bring something different and something unique to the union. We've come to recognize that our differences make us stronger together. *"If the whole body were an eye, where would the sense of hearing be?"*[1] So, you must ask yourself: "Can I love and accept this person exactly as they are?" If the answer is no, it may be best to walk away rather than enter a lifelong relationship expecting a transformation that may never happen.

A strong marriage begins with a wise choice. Do not allow external pressures, cultural expectations, fleeting emotions, or the opinions of others to dictate your decision. While these

---

[1] 1st Corinthians 12:17

factors may hold some significance, they should not be the ultimate determining factors in choosing a life partner. People change—both physically and psychologically. Even if you date for years or live together before marriage (which we do not advocate), you cannot fully predict how someone will evolve over the next 20 years. Sometimes, even after decades together, we still surprise each other! However, God is all-knowing. He sees what we cannot. He knows what is best for you and what you can and cannot handle. Do not rely solely on your own understanding—trust in the One who sees all things.[2] Seek His guidance, and He will lead you to the right person, ensuring that your marriage is built on a firm and lasting foundation.

Before You Say 'I Do' — Application Steps

While no couple will agree on every single topic, it is crucial to align on core values and fundamental beliefs. It is very difficult to "do life" with someone whose map of the world and values are completely different to yours. Before you commit to a lifetime together here are some essential questions to ask:

☑ Do we share the same beliefs and spiritual foundation?

☑ Do we agree on the key values that will shape our marriage and family?

---

[2] Proverbs 3:5-6

☑ Do they bring out the best in me, or do they trigger my worst tendencies?

☑ Do they truly love, honour and respect me?

☑ Do I find myself constantly making excuses for their behaviour?

☑ Do we share the same vision and purpose for marriage?

☑ Do I truly love and accept them for who they are, not what I hope they will become?

2

CHOOSE COMMITMENT OVER CONVENIENCE

Staying the Course When Love Feels Like Work

You've probably heard the phrase *"Till death do us part"* recited at countless weddings. We remember saying those very words ourselves, standing before God, our family, and friends. They weren't just part of a script—they were a heartfelt promise. A mutual vow that said, *"We're in this for life."*

But let's be honest—we live in a world where commitment is rare. Choices are often made based on fleeting feelings or convenience. People say, *"Life's too short,"* and jump from one relationship to another at the first sign of discomfort—only to repeat the same cycle. Sadly, many carry this mindset into marriage, treating it like a temporary arrangement rather than a lifelong covenant. It's no wonder so many marriages fall apart just months, or even week after they begin.

The truth is, if you're not ready to commit to the long haul, you're not ready to get married. Marriage is not a sprint; it's a marathon. It requires much more than emotions. It demands a decision—a choice to stay. Right from the beginning, both partners must enter with the mindset that there's no back door. No plan B. No exit strategy.

Burn Your Bridges

Too often, people walk into marriage with one foot already out the door. They say, *"I'll try this for a few years and see how it goes. If it doesn't meet my expectations, I'm out."* But that mindset sets the stage for failure before the marriage even begins. Marriage requires a "burn the-bridges" kind of commitment. The kind that says, *"This will work, or this will work."* If both partners embrace this attitude and are willing to do the work—we'll explore this more in a later chapter—the marriage is bound to thrive.

Before we got married, we both knew we were choosing a lifelong journey of oneness. There was no going back. It wasn't "sink or swim"—it was *"swim or swim."* We were deeply in love and committed to each other, but we also knew love alone wouldn't carry us through. We expected challenges—we just didn't know how many or how often. And we were right! We've had our fair share of bumps along the way, but through it all, we've remained committed not just to ensuring our marriage endures, but t ensuring it is enjoyed. We're in it—for life.

Build on Something Unshaking

Our faith has been a cornerstone of that commitment. We believe that marriage is a sacred covenant between a man and a woman, a divine joining that goes far beyond romance. The Bible tells us that God hates divorce[3]—not because He wants people trapped in unhappy marriages, but because He knows the pain it causes; to the couple, to the children, and to the families around them. God desires that we work on our marriages, and with His help, we truly can make them work.

Beyond our faith, we also understand that our marriage impacts more than just the two of us. Our choices ripple outward—to our dear children, who mean the world to us, our extended families, those we lead, and the many who look up to us. This awareness has fuelled our resolve and pushed us to go beyond ourselves and only what we want, to investing deeply in the success of our marriage.

It's Not Just About You; There is More at Stake

We'll never forget a powerful moment during Julius' 50th birthday celebration. Our eldest son, who was 17 at the time, performed a spoken word piece in honour of his dad. He

---

[3] Malachi 2:16

opened with the line: *"My father is not a rolling stone; he's a solid rock that stayed in our home."* Those words moved us deeply. In that simple yet profound tribute, he captured the lasting impact of commitment and presence.

Having seen friends whose fathers had walked away—leaving behind broken homes and hurting hearts—our son knew the value of a dad who stayed. His words were not just a celebration of his father, but a powerful reminder that the choices we make in our marriage ripple outward, shaping the lives of those who look up to us. Commitment isn't just about the two of you—it's about everyone your love and presence touches.

It's easy to talk about love and commitment when everything is going smoothly. But the true test comes when life gets hard. In today's culture, it's tempting to choose convenience over perseverance. When things get difficult, people walk away instead of working through the hard stuff. But every marriage will face pressures—whether it's finances, health issues, parenting struggles, or career challenges. The question is: how will you face them together? In those tough seasons, return to your "why." Why did you commit to each other in the first place? What hopes and dreams did you share at the beginning? Revisit those moments. Remind each other of what brought you together—and choose to keep fighting for it.

Marriage is not 50/50

A crucial part of commitment is embracing the truth that marriage isn't 50/50. It's 100/100. You both must be all in. Anything less leaves too much room for imbalance and sets the marriage up for failure. Marriage means putting *"we"* before *"me."* Every decision, every sacrifice, every act of love must serve the whole, not just the individual.

It also means accepting that neither of you is perfect. You will make mistakes. You will disappoint each other. But understanding this makes room for grace. You must learn to forgive quickly, extend understanding, and move forward—over and over again. Forgiveness isn't always easy, but it's absolutely essential. Holding on to hurt only poisons your connection. Let go of grudges. Choose grace. You'll need it—and so will your spouse. We expand on this in a subsequent chapter.

We've had our fair share of tough times—moments when walking away seemed easier than pressing on. We're not here to paint a perfect picture. Marriage is for grown-ups. In many ways, our marriage has been like a bed of roses—beautiful, yes, but not without thorns. We've faced challenges in raising children, navigating financial setbacks, business failures, career shifts, and the unique pressures of ministry. But through it all—by God's grace—we have held on.

We chose to stay committed. Not because it was always easy. But because it was *worth it.*

Choose Commitment Over Convenience — Application Steps

Commitment is not just a word but a verb, so actions are required from both of you. You must be intentional and willing to invest in your marriage, together. Here are some practical steps you can take to strengthen your commitment to each other and your union:

☑ **Revisit Your Vows** — Take time to read through your wedding vows together. Discuss what they mean to you now and how you can continue living them out daily; this can be a powerful way for both of you to reconnect with your promises and reaffirm your shared commitment.

☑ **Serve Each Other** — Look for ways to serve your spouse as much as possible. Offer to do a chore they dislike, make them their favourite meal, or offer a listening ear when they are having a bad day. Acts of service demonstrate your love and commitment tangibly to one another.

☑ **Seek Support When Needed** — If you are facing challenges in your marriage, don't be afraid to seek help from a trusted counsellor. A neutral third party can help you navigate difficult times and find solutions that work for both of you.

3

START WITH THE END IN MIND

Have a Clear Vision For Your Family

Have you ever tried setting out on a journey without knowing exactly where you were going? That's what it's like entering marriage or building a family without a clear vision—it's like driving without a map. You might move, but you'll likely end up somewhere you never intended. As with any meaningful journey, you need a destination in mind.

In marriage, vision is not optional—it's essential. And it's not just any vision, but a shared one. A vision that unites both partners and gives direction to the family you're building together. Without it, you may find yourselves drifting—not only aimlessly, but possibly apart. Vision gives clarity. It helps you align your decisions, set your priorities, and measure your progress. As the Bible reminds us, "Where there is no vision, the people perish."[4]

_____

[4] Proverbs 29:18

When we were preparing for marriage, we sat down and talked seriously about the kind of family we wanted to build. We discussed our values, our dreams, the kind of home we hoped to raise our children in, and what we both saw as success—not just career-wise, but in terms of the kind of life and legacy we wanted to create. That conversation became our compass. Our shared vision helped us stay connected and make decisions intentionally, even when life got overwhelming.

Vision Keeps You Focused and United

One of the greatest benefits of having a shared vision is the unity it creates. It becomes much easier to detect distractions, recognize red flags, and say "no" to anything that doesn't align with your goals. It's like having your family's destination pinned on a map— you might still take detours or hit a few bumps along the road, but you're always aware of where you're heading. If you're already married and you haven't yet developed a clear family vision, it's not too late. The best time to start was yesterday, but the next best time is today. Sit down together and start asking the big questions. What matters to us? What are we trying to build? What do we want our children to say about this home one day?

Laying the Groundwork: Define Your Core Values

Your vision is only as strong as the foundation it's built on— and that foundation is made up of your core values. Think of your family as a tree. The values you share are the roots. They ground you, nourish you, and help you grow strong and steady through every season. Start by asking yourselves: What do we believe in? What values matter most to us? Is it faith? Integrity? Love? Service? Honesty? Growth? Legacy?

These core values become the lens through which you view decisions, the filter for your choices, and the glue that holds you together when life gets messy. Let's be honest: no couple agrees on everything. And that's okay. The key is to find common ground— the values you both hold dear and build from there. The rest, you'll learn to work through together.

Two of our most cherished core values are faith and family, and we are intentional about ensuring nothing compromises them. We've turned down lucrative job offers—not because we didn't need the money, but because they clashed with these priorities. One particular opportunity required Julius to work away from home for extended periods, which would have effectively made him a remote husband and father. With our children still very young at the time, we knew that wasn't the kind of family life we envisioned. Saying no wasn't difficult because we viewed the decision through the lens of our values—and it simply didn't align. Because we had already defined our values long before the opportunity came, making the decision was much easier. We encourage you to do the same—establish your values early, so they can guide you when tough choices arise.

Create a Family Mission Statement:

Your Shared Compass

A family mission statement is a short, clear declaration of your shared purpose and direction. It's the heartbeat of your vision— something you can return to in moments of confusion, conflict, or major decision-making. Don't overthink it. A mission statement could be as simple as *"We are a family committed to faith, love, growth, and service. We will build a home where every person is seen, heard, and valued. Together, we will pursue purpose, support one another, and leave a legacy of integrity and impact."* Write it down. Put it where you can see it—on the wall, the fridge, your phones. And revisit it often. As your family grows and seasons change, update it to reflect your current vision.

Set Goals That Bring the Vision to Life

Having a vision is powerful, but it needs structure. That's where goal setting comes in. Goals turn your shared dreams into clear action steps. Consider the different areas of your life together—spiritual, financial, relational, personal growth, health, parenting, community involvement—and set intentional goals in each one. You've probably heard of the SMART acronym as it relates to goal setting. Make sure your goal is:

- **Specific –** Define clearly what you want to do.

- **Measurable** – Make sure progress can be tracked.

- **Achievable** – Be realistic.

- **Relevant** – Align goals with your vision and values.

- **Time-bound** – Set deadlines to keep you focused.

For example, instead of "We want more quality time," you might say, "We'll have a no-devices family dinner at least four nights a week." or, "We'll save X amount for a family vacation by 31st December." The more intentional and specific you are, the more momentum you'll build.

Leave a Legacy with Your Vision

When you build your family with a clear, shared vision, you're not just planning for the next year—you're shaping generations. Your children and those watching you will learn what commitment, unity, and purpose look like by watching you live it out. We can tell you from experience that working toward a shared vision has strengthened our bond, anchored our decisions, and helped us persevere through challenges. It's not always been easy, but it's always been worth it. We've watched our children grow up with a sense of identity, direction, and belonging—and that, to us, is legacy. So, as you build your home, we encourage you, don't just hope for a great marriage or a strong family. Design it. Speak it. Write it down and work towards it—together.

Start With the End in Mind — Application Steps

☑ **Have a Vision Casting Date Night** — Set aside an evening to dream together. Turn off all distractions. Talk about your hopes for your marriage, your children (or future children), your home environment, and the kind of impact you want to have as a family. What kind of family do you want to build? If someone described your home 10 or 20 years from now, what would you want them to say?

☑ **Define Your Core Values** — Each party should list their top five core values. Then, compare your lists, discuss why each value matters to you, and highlight any shared values. This simple yet powerful exercise can deepen your understanding of each other in meaningful ways. When we guide couples and teams through a Values Discovery Session, it's always eye-opening. If you'd like support in uncovering your values, feel free to reach out—we'd be glad to help.

☑ **Create a Family Mission Statement** — Use your vision and core values to craft a short mission statement. Keep it under 100 words. Post it somewhere visible and review it together at least twice a year to keep it alive and relevant.

4

WORK ON THE RELATIONSHIP

Staying Married Requires More
Than Just Staying Together

Like we've already said, commitment is the foundation of any successful relationship—especially marriage. It's what sets marriage apart from other relationships. By definition, marriage is a lifelong commitment to another person. But as crucial as commitment is, commitment alone is not enough to sustain a happy, thriving marriage.

Two people can be deeply committed to their marriage—choosing to stay together no matter the challenges—yet still end up in an unhappy, unfulfilling relationship. Some couples may choose to remain married for reasons beyond their own happiness—perhaps out of duty to their children, their role as spiritual or community leaders, or the desire to set a good example for others.

As noble as these motivations are, they are not enough to create a truly joyful and satisfying marriage. Beyond commitment, both partners must be willing to put in the work. Without this effort, a marriage can last for decades but feel lifeless and empty—two people sharing the same space but emotionally disconnected.

Marriage Requires Continuous Effort

As a solicitor, Mary practiced family and matrimonial law for several years, and time and again, saw couples who had been married for 30 or even 40 years—decades of shared history—suddenly seeking a divorce. From the outside, you might assume that if they had made it that far, they were in it for the long haul. But the reality was often different. Many of these couples had stopped investing in their relationship long before. They stayed together out of duty—perhaps to provide a stable home for their children—but once the children grew up and left, they realized there was nothing left holding them together.

This phenomenon, often referred to as **"grey divorce,"** is on the rise. While divorce rates among younger adults have declined, those aged 50 and older are divorcing at twice the rate they did in the 1990s, and it's projected to triple by 2030. (Stepler, 2017) In the UK where we live, nearly **44%** of marriages end in divorce by their 30th anniversary. (Yurday, April 2024) This raises an important question: Why are so many long-term marriages falling apart? There are several reasons for divorce in later life.

Growing Apart

The number one reason for grey divorce is couples growing apart. In the early years, life is often filled with responsibilities—building careers, raising children, and managing a busy household. Many couples unintentionally neglect their own relationship while focusing on these demands. When the children leave home—the "glue" that held them together—they suddenly realize they have hardly anything in common anymore. But children and careers aren't the only causes of drifting apart. If one person invests in their personal growth while the other remains stagnant, their perspectives and priorities can diverge significantly over time.

Years of Unresolved Issues

Many couples avoid conflict rather than resolving it. They may argue frequently in the early years, but over time, one or both partners stop trying—not because the issues are resolved, but because they're exhausted. Unspoken disappointments, unmet needs (both emotional and physical), and years of emotional disconnection accumulate like a ticking time bomb. Some stay together out of duty, suppressing their unhappiness. But when the distractions of parenting or careers fade, those long-buried resentments surface, leading to the decision to walk away.

Different Life Goals and Priorities

People are living longer than ever, and with that longevity comes a re-evaluation of life's priorities. What once seemed like a shared vision may no longer align. One spouse may want to travel the world, while the other longs for a quiet, routine life. One may feel energized by new adventures, while the other prefers slowing down. Retirement can also bring different expectations. While one person sees it as a time of rest, another might view it as a chance to pursue old dreams. When visions and priorities clash, couples may feel they've grown too far apart to continue together.

The Strain of Health Challenges

Longer life expectancy means many couples face serious health challenges together. Physical and mental health struggles can put immense pressure on a marriage. Chronic illness or mobility issues may change the dynamics of the relationship, shifting one partner into a caregiver role, which could lead to resentment or avoidance. The loss of physical intimacy due to menopause, erectile dysfunction, or illness can also create emotional distance, often contributing to infidelity in the marriage. Without open communication and mutual support, health challenges can drive a wedge between even the strongest couples.

Divorce is NOT the Answer

Every question has an answer, and every problem has a solution— divorce doesn't have to be one of them. When weighing your options, make a conscious effort to keep divorce off the table, allowing yourself the chance to explore solutions that may not be immediately obvious but could ultimately be the best path forward. God desires for your marriage to thrive, and if BOTH of you are committed to doing the work, He will guide and help you every step of the way.

Staying Together Requires Effort

We truly believe that God's vision for marriage is not just about staying together but about experiencing true unity and oneness.[5] And while it takes work, we also know that any relationship can thrive when BOTH partners are willing to invest in it. Have we ever had seasons where we thought parting ways would be easier? Absolutely!! But we knew that divorce wasn't the real solution—it would just mean carrying our unresolved struggles into another relationship, hoping it works next time. As John C. Maxwell says, "Hope is not a strategy." You can't just hope your marriage will thrive. You have to be intentional about nurturing it.

---

[5] Genesis 2:24

A happy, fulfilling marriage is like a garden. if you do nothing, weeds—resentment, distance, neglect—will take over. But if you are intentional in sowing the right seeds and you water, and cultivate it with care, you'll enjoy the beauty and fruit of your labour. Your relationship is no different. You can't expect to spend all your time at work, or attending to the children, your business, ministry or anything else and expect that because you live under the same roof and see each other every day, your relationship will blossom. It takes more than that. It takes intentionality, it takes time, and it takes effort, but it is so well worth it. You are both so well worth it!

Work on The Relationship—Application Steps

☑ **Prioritize quality time**—date nights, shared hobbies, and meaningful conversations. Be intentional about maintaining intimacy, both physical and emotional. You might not always feel like it, but prioritizing connection strengthens the bond.

☑ **Don't avoid hard conversations**—address issues early and honestly, even if it's uncomfortable. Never stop communicating. It might often feel like déjà vu, but if it's still an issue, don't ever stop trying to resolve it.

☑ **Regularly discuss your future**—dream together and plan together. Two can't walk together unless they are agreed.[6]

---

[6] Amos 3:3

If you stay curious about each other, then your spouse's dreams and goals should come as no surprise to you in your later years.

☑ **Prioritize healthy living**—encourage each other to exercise, eat well, and get regular check-ups. It's all about being intentional. Discuss long-term care and expectations and make joint decisions about them.

5

WORK ON YOURSELF

Every Partnership is Only as Strong as the Individual Partners

A strong and thriving marriage doesn't just happen—it's built on the foundation of two individuals who are continually growing, evolving, and striving to be their best selves. Too often, people enter marriage expecting their partner to complete them, fulfil their every need, or be the solution to their personal struggles. But the truth is, no relationship can rise above the strength and maturity of the individuals within it.

As much as we all like to think that we are perfect and if everyone could be like us the world would be a perfect place, nothing could be further from the truth. You are not perfect in fact if everyone was like you the world would be a very difficult place to live in. The problem is we cannot see the picture when we are in the frame. We once heard the story of a man who had three accidents in one day and at the end of the day in exasperation exclaimed, "what's the matter with all these drivers?!" Laughable right? but it's so easy to fall into the trap of thinking the problem is all with everyone else.

In the words of James Allen, the author of the book As a Man Thinketh,

> "Men are anxious to improve their circumstances but are unwilling to improve themselves; they therefore remain bound. The man who does not shrink from self-crucifixion can never fail to accomplish the object upon which his heart is set."

This is a powerful life transforming thought. We're often tempted to think if only this, that, or the other would change in our lives everything would be perfect. If only our spouse would be more understanding, if only our boss would be more accommodating, if only our children would be more respectful and on and on it goes. The list of 'if onlys' just gets longer and longer. The reality is, even if those circumstances around us changed they would only be replaced by a different set of circumstances, and we find ourselves perpetually bound in this circle of wishing and wanting to change or control things that are completely outside of our control. What James Allen is propounding instead is to do the work that really matters, the work that produces enduring change and that is the work we do on ourselves. When we change, everything in our lives will change.

It is not uncommon for people to end up with a 2nd, or 3rd and sometimes even 4th marriage because they are caught in the illusion of trying to find the perfect partner. They are like the man who had three accidents in one day and wondered why every other driver is such a poor driver. Without working on yourself, you mentally transfer your struggles and your own shortcomings into the next relationship.

Of course there are instances of people making their second marriage work. We believe this is only because they learned their lessons from the first. If you don't, a new partner alone will not solve the problem because you are part of the problem. So why not learn the lesson with the partner you're with right now so you can both build a happy marriage together and save yourselves, your children and everyone else involved the heartache and huge expense of divorce? Stop trying to change or control others. Change and control the one person that you can—yourself.

Three key areas in which you must work on yourself to build a thriving marriage:

We believe there are 3 core aspects to every human being: the physical, the spiritual, and the intellectual, and to bring our best selves to our relationship we must be prepared to work on each of these areas.

Spiritual Development—Strengthening Your Marriage From the Inside Out

Marriage is more than just a legal or emotional partnership—it is a sacred union that requires more than love and compatibility to thrive. For us, our Christian faith has been the foundation of our marriage. The Bible is our final arbiter, meaning we don't allow our emotions, no matter how strong, or our wisdom, no matter how great we think it is, to dictate how we run our home. Instead, we trust in a higher, wiser, and more perfect authority—God. And we can honestly say that putting Jesus at the centre of our marriage has been the *secret sauce* that has kept our union strong, even through the most challenging seasons.

Spiritual growth is not just about personal faith; it deeply impacts how we relate to others. Growing spiritually, allows our faith to shape our character, guide our decisions, and influence the way we love and serve each other. There are many aspects of spiritual growth that we consider to be very important, but three that have proven vital in our journey are *forgiveness, self-sacrifice,* and *seeking wisdom and power beyond ourselves.* We delve deeper into all three in other chapters.

Physical Appearance—Taking Care of Yourself

It's no secret that physical attraction plays a major role in relationships, and while love may run deeper than appearances, the way we take care of ourselves speaks volumes about the value we place on our marriage. Too often, couples grow comfortable—sometimes too comfortable—taking each other for granted and neglecting the effort they once put into looking and feeling their best. But here's the truth: caring for your physical well-being isn't just about looking good for your spouse; it's about maintaining confidence, energy, and vitality that enhance every aspect of your relationship. Here are three ways you can invest in your physical development.

Prioritizing Exercise and Healthy Habits: A thriving marriage needs energy, and a healthy body helps sustain it. Regular exercise reduces stress, lifts your mood, and builds confidence—all of which positively affect your relationship. It's not about chasing a six-pack, but about being your best self. Whether it's walking together, dancing, or hitting the gym, staying active benefits both you and your marriage. Healthy eating plays a key role, too. There's a saying in Africa that a good wife gives her husband what he wants to eat— something Julius would often joke about when craving fried food. Mary's classic response? "A good wife gives her husband what's good for him to eat." 😊 It's all about making nourishing choices that support long-term well-being.

Maintaining Physical Appeal: During dating, most people put in serious effort to look their best—so why should that stop after marriage? Often, people revamp their appearance only after a breakup. But your spouse deserves the best version of you now, not after things fall apart. Looking after your appearance isn't about vanity; it's a sign of respect for both you and your partner. It means showing you still care by staying well-groomed, dressing thoughtfully, and taking pride in how you present yourself. The same energy you gave while dating should carry on well beyond the "I do."

Personal Hygiene: It may seem basic, but poor hygiene can be a major romance killer. Small things—fresh breath, clean clothes, and a quick shower—make a big difference. Smelling like dinner or showing up unkempt can quickly dim physical attraction. Good hygiene isn't just about looking or smelling nice—it's about showing care and respect for your partner. A little effort in this area goes a long way in keeping the spark alive.

Personal Development—Investing in Your Own Personal Growth

If there is one investment that has had the greatest impact on our relationship, it is the investment we have made in our personal growth. Many people mistakenly equate personal development with professional development, but they are fundamentally different. While professional growth focuses on improving skills that enhance your career—such as a solicitor attending legal training—personal growth is about investing in yourself as an individual, regardless of your profession. It is what shapes your character, refines your mindset, and ultimately determines how you navigate relationships, including marriage.

The way you think, communicate, handle conflict, and regulate your emotions directly affects the health of your relationship.

No matter how deeply you love each other, if one person frequently lashes out in anger, or struggles with effective communication, that love will eventually become buried under resentment and strife. Personal development is not just about bettering yourself—it is about strengthening your ability to build and sustain a fulfilling, lasting marriage. There are many aspects of personal growth one could embark on, but three essential areas that significantly impact a relationship are *emotional maturity, a growth mindset, and a positive attitude.*

Emotional Maturity: Learning to Manage, Not Just Express, Your Emotions

One of the greatest tests of character in marriage is how you handle your emotions. Feelings are powerful, and when not managed well, they can wreak havoc on a relationship. Emotional maturity is not about suppressing emotions but about learning to *respond* rather than *react.* When a partner frequently loses control, says hurtful things in the heat of the moment, or holds onto grudges, the emotional toll on the relationship is immense. On the other hand, a spouse who has the ability to process emotions in a healthy way, learning to pause before reacting, creates a safe and nurturing environment for the marriage to thrive.

A Growth Mindset: The Commitment to Continual Self-Improvement

Having a growth mindset means being open to learning, reading, and seeking knowledge that helps you become a better person and a better spouse. It means adopting a 'life-long learner' mentality and embracing every challenge as an opportunity for growth. It is the ability to recognize your flaws and work on them rather than making excuses, blaming others for them or expecting your partner to simply accept them. When both partners are committed to cultivating a growth mindset, they bring fresh energy, wisdom, and resilience into the marriage. They challenge each other to grow and build a relationship that is continuously evolving rather than deteriorating over time.

Attitude: The Altitude of Your Marriage Depends on it

Your attitude plays a major role in shaping the health and direction of your marriage. It influences how you view your spouse, navigate challenges, and respond to everyday life. A negative attitude focuses on flaws, complaints, and obstacles—making the relationship feel draining instead of life-giving. A positive attitude, however, sees potential over problems. It means highlighting your spouse's strengths, choosing grace over criticism, and creating a supportive, hopeful environment.

It doesn't ignore difficulties—it meets them with resilience and belief in your shared future.

Marriage isn't just about finding the right person—it's about becoming the right person. When you commit to personal growth, you bring your best self to the relationship. That's one of the greatest gifts you can give your spouse: a healthier, stronger, evolving version of you.

Work on Yourself—Application Steps

☑ **Prioritize a shared spiritual foundation –** If faith is important in your relationship, set aside time to pray together, study scripture, and align your values based on shared beliefs. Let go of grudges quickly. Don't go to sleep without making up, even if it means making the first move, and even when you know you have done nothing wrong.

☑ **Take care of your body –** Take up one form of exercise you can commit to doing at least weekly. If it's something you can do together, even better, you'll be killing two birds with one stone. Keeping fit and staying connected.

☑ **Read and keep learning –** Choose one area of growth— It could be managing your emotions, practicing active listening or guarding your tongue under pressure—and commit to growing in that area. Read books, watch YouTube videos, attend courses—get intentional in growing in that area.

6

START EACH DAY ANEW

Let Go of the Past and Keep Letting Go

One of the greatest challenges in any relationship is the ability to truly forgive and let go of past hurts. No matter how much love exists between two people, there will always be moments of disappointment, misunderstanding, and pain. However, what determines the strength and longevity of a marriage is not the absence of these hurts, but the ability to fully release them and start each day with a clean slate.

It's human nature to remember pain. We don't wake up every day with amnesia, forgetting everything that has ever been said or done to hurt us. But while we may not forget, we can choose not to carry yesterday's wounds into today. If we don't, our relationship becomes weighed down by an ever-growing list of offenses, and eventually, the burden becomes too heavy to bear.

The Apostle Paul captured this principle beautifully in the bible when he said, *"One thing I do: Forgetting what is behind and straining toward what is ahead, I press on toward the goal."*[7] Remember the goal in marriage is perfect unity. Imagine trying to drive forward while keeping your eyes fixed on the rearview mirror—you will inevitably crash. In the same way, constantly looking back at past offenses will hinder the progress of your marriage. Now, we have to make clear that letting go is not about pretending nothing happened, nor is it about suppressing emotions. Instead, it's about making a conscious decision to release past wounds, so they no longer dictate the future.

The Danger of Holding On

When we hold on to resentment, we begin to build walls—not just between ourselves and our spouse but also around our own hearts. Initially, these walls feel like protection, shielding us from further pain. However, over time, they become prisons, locking us in isolation and preventing true intimacy. A marriage cannot thrive when one or both partners are emotionally guarded. Love flourishes in an atmosphere of trust and vulnerability.[8] Trust cannot exist where past mistakes are constantly being revisited.

Rehashing past hurts can also create a toxic cycle where one partner constantly feels punished for mistakes they have

---

[7] Philippians 3:13-14
[8] Genesis 2:25

already repented of. This leads to frustration, discouragement, and ultimately emotional withdrawal. If your spouse feels that no matter what they do, they will always be defined by their past failures, they may stop trying altogether. Instead of working to improve the relationship, they may feel trapped in a dynamic where forgiveness is spoken but never truly given.

What Does True Letting Go Look Like?

Letting go does not mean ignoring problems or sweeping issues under the rug. Some wounds take time to heal, and some conflicts require deeper conversations before they can be resolved. However, once forgiveness has been given, it should be complete. That means:

No keeping score – Bringing up past mistakes in every disagreement is a sign that forgiveness was not fully extended. Keep no record of wrongs.[9]

No silent punishments – Forgiveness means we stop making our spouse "pay" for what they did through passive-aggressive behaviour, coldness, or withholding affection.

No bringing up old wounds to win arguments – If you have forgiven, leave the past where it belongs. Focus on resolving current issues based on the present facts rather than allowing past failures to shape your perceptions, attitude, or

---

[9] 1st Corinthians 13:5

response. The way we choose to see a situation influences how we react and holding onto past mistakes can distort our view and prevent genuine resolution.

No building walls – True forgiveness means remaining open, vulnerable, and trusting again, even when it feels risky.

Here are some **Practical Steps to Letting Go**

Decide in advance to forgive: Don't wait until emotions run high. Make forgiveness your default posture so that when offenses happen, your heart is already prepared to release them. Choose to extend grace rather than insisting on justice. Just as your spouse will hurt you at times, you will also hurt them, and we are sure when that happens you will want grace extended to you. So, remembering your own imperfections should make it easier to extend grace. Try to resolve any unresolved issues before you go to sleep.[10]

Communicate openly and constantly: If something is bothering you, address it promptly and constructively rather than letting resentment to fester. At times, it may feel like you're repeating yourself, and the thought might creep in: *"I've brought this up so many times, we've had this conversation over and over, yet nothing changes."* Or *"If my spouse truly loved me, they would have changed by now, given how often we've discussed this."* We admit, it can

---

[10] Ephesians 4:26

be exhausting, but what's the alternative? Unresolved pain doesn't just disappear—it hardens into bitterness.

Pray for your spouse: It is hard to stay resentful toward someone you consistently pray for; not necessarily for God to change them—although that is not a bad prayer to pray as long as we are not approaching it from a holier than thou posture thinking you are perfect and your spouse alone needs some work—rather ask God to help you see them through His eyes. We can guarantee God is not thinking some of the things you are thinking about your spouse 😊

Seek help when needed – If you are really struggling to let go of deep hurts, counselling or pastoral guidance can provide support and tools to help you move forward. You don't have to walk the road alone, seek professional help if you need it.

Letting go is not a one-time event but a daily decision. Choose to start every day fresh, not as a couple weighed down by the past, but as two people who are committed to building a future together—free, unburdened, and full of love. This is the power of letting go!

Start Every Day Anew - Application Steps

☑ **Foster Psychological Safety –** Create an environment where your spouse feels safe to express concerns and talk about anything they are unhappy with, without fear of judgment or making things worse. Regularly reassure them that they can openly share their feelings with you and communicate your commitment to responding with understanding rather than defensiveness—and be sure to live up to that commitment.

☑ **Create a Letting-Go Routine –** Whether it's ending the day with prayer, journaling, or simply affirming to yourself, *"I choose to release today's hurts and start afresh tomorrow,"* develop a habit that helps you consciously let go of grievances and renew your commitment to your marriage each day.

☑ **Use a Physical Action to Symbolize Letting Go –** Find a tangible way to release resentment, such as writing down grievances and then tearing up the paper, taking a deep breath and exhaling negativity, or physically shaking off tension. Associating a physical action with emotional release helps reinforce the commitment to start fresh.

7

BE EACH OTHER'S BIGGEST CHEERLEADERS

Supporting and Celebrating Each Other's Dreams and Wins

One essential 'tool' you cannot do without in your marital toolkit is being your spouse's strongest cheerleader. We are not talking about casual or passive support here, but actively encouraging, celebrating, and cheering each other on as you pursue your dreams and aspirations. Subtle competition can arise when couples try to outdo each other instead of working together. Here's the truth: You can't build a strong partnership if you're in silent competition. Marriage is a team sport. Your spouse's victory is your victory. Their success becomes part of your shared legacy.

The worst thing you can do in a marriage is create separate territories, with each party building their own separate empires, when you should be building a shared life together. If you fail to grasp the true essence of marriage, it's quite easy to fall into this pattern. We must remember that the goal of marriage is oneness.

While it is important to maintain our unique individuality, we must not fail to realise that our true strength as a couple lies in building together as a unit. In this atmosphere of togetherness, you begin to thrive and soar as a couple. One is too small a number to achieve anything of significance. Every great accomplishment in life requires teamwork, and who better to have on your team than your spouse? Marriage should be a sanctuary where a collaborative spirit replaces all competitiveness. In this setting, competition transforms into completion, working together to achieve more.

The Shift from Competition to Completion

In marriage, we do not compete against each other; instead, we complete each other! In other words, we achieve better results by working together, supporting each other's endeavours. The paradigm shift from competition to completion acknowledges that both partners bring unique strengths and talents to the union and working together in the spirit of perfect harmony, you become unstoppable!

In our home, for example, we understand that each other's success is *our* success, so we never hesitate to support and cheer each other along fully. Think of it this way: a garden flourishes when each plant receives adequate sunlight, water, and care. In a marriage, we are each other's gardeners, nurturing the seeds of potential and growth.

We operate as one, because we know we are a team! We often discuss what we are working on or projects we are thinking of embarking on, allowing each other to look at it with fresh eyes and objectively voice their thoughts. Once we agree, that is it! We may not physically do 'it' together, but whatever 'it' is becomes "our" project. We share the burdens and celebrate the wins together. We would often discuss the struggles and challenges because a burden shared is a burden half solved, right? Then we will hold our mini 'mastermind' sessions, bouncing ideas off each other, and praying together, because when one wins, we both win!

We honestly couldn't do even half of what we do without each other's unwavering support. We truly are each other's biggest cheerleaders. When I hesitated and procrastinated about launching my law firm, Julius gently reminded me of the dream I had shared with him back when we first met, and his encouragement gave me the courage to move forward. Also, when I made the bold decision to transition from law into the world of training and development, he stood right there beside me—cheering me on, believing in me, and pushing me to soar. He wants to see me succeed just as much, if not more, as I want to succeed.

Similarly with running a global organisation and pastoring a church, Mary's unwavering support has been absolutely priceless. She is 100% committed to the ministry and always challenges and encourages me to keep going and on days when it just seems like the best thing to do is to pack it all in, her strong, confident voice telling me "you can, and you will" gives me the strength to keep moving forward. Every now and then, I get inspired with entrepreneurial ideas or side hustles, and Mary is always there—not just with wise counsel, but with hands-on support whenever it's needed. I really couldn't ask for a better teammate and life partner. As the Bible reminds us, two is better than one, because when one falls, the other can lift them up It really is unfortunate if you are alone when you fall, as you have no one to help you. [11]

Encouragement has the power to make people thrive. It uplifts, energises, and unlocks potential—while criticism and discouragement quietly drain the spark from even the strongest hearts. Make it a habit to celebrate each other's wins, no matter how small they may seem. Every achievement, from landing a new client to finally finishing that DIY project, is a moment worth acknowledging. A simple, heartfelt *"Well done, love—that was amazing"* can go a long way in fuelling confidence and connection.

When you choose to be each other's biggest cheerleader, your relationship benefits far beyond the moment. You build trust, deepen your bond, and create a culture of mutual admiration. Over time, this steady rhythm of encouragement becomes the heartbeat of your relationship—a safe, joy-filled space where

---

[11] Ecclesiastes 4:9-12

love grows, support flows freely, and victories are always shared. It's not just about what you achieve, but how you lift each other as you do it together. That's the kind of love that stands the test of time

Be Each Other's Biggest Cheerleaders—Application Steps

☑ **Specific Praise**—Avoid giving vague compliments to each other. Make note of something specific you admire about your spouse and tell them. It could be something they said, the way they handled a situation, or a goal achieved. Spell it out!

☑ **Actively Listen**— When your partner shares their dreams or concerns, give them your full attention. Put the phone down, step away from distractions, and truly listen. Your presence shows you care—and helps you catch those meaningful moments where encouragement, praise, or support can make all the difference.

☑ **Offer Practical Help**—Sometimes, cheering means rolling up your sleeves and offering practical assistance to each other. Ask your spouse how you can better support them. It could be helping out with the admin in the business, taking on extra chores, or helping them to design their publicity materials if you are creative in that area. These acts of service demonstrate your commitment and support.

☑ **Celebrate Milestones**—Consider marking significant achievements with a celebration together! It does not need to be something big but do something to celebrate. It could be a special dinner, a bunch of flowers, or a heartfelt card to show your partner how much you value their accomplishment.

8

DO LIFE SIDE BY SIDE NOT MILES APART

Intentionally Creating Shared Memories

Having a shared vision is vital for any thriving marriage. But here's the truth: a shared vision without a strong emotional connection can leave you feeling more like business partners than life partners. We've all seen couples who have built empires or chased careers, only to find their family life falling to pieces behind the scenes. They may have gained success, but somewhere along the line, they lost each other. Don't fall into the same trap.

An emotionally connected couple is the heartbeat of a successful family. These bonds aren't built on grand gestures but through intentional, everyday moments of presence and participation. It's about being fully engaged—emotionally, mentally, and physically. Whether it's cooking together, going for a walk, or watching a documentary side by side, the key word is together.

In the early days of our relationship, doing life together came naturally. We shared similar values and interests, so most of our time outside work was spent side by side. We'd even wait for each other to eat, no matter how long it took. We were inseparable—and honestly, we still are.

Looking back, we treasure those organic moments. They helped lay the foundation for the deep connection we now enjoy. But life changes. Children arrive, responsibilities grow, and schedules tighten. That's when we learned the power of intentionality. These days, we have to *choose* to make space for each other, to plan activities, and to create fresh memories that keep our bond alive and evolving.

Nurturing the Bond Through Shared Connection

Think of your family life as a garden. It needs care—water, sunlight, and nourishment. Each interaction, no matter how small, is a drop of life that helps your relationship bloom. Whether it's a family bike ride, a puzzle on the weekend, or attending a local event, these shared experiences deepen your bond in beautiful, often unexpected ways.

We don't have a perfect record, and yes, we wish we'd done even more. But we're incredibly grateful for the memories we have—and we continue to create new ones. Here are some **Practical Pathways to Creating Connections** that's really helped us.

Treasure Mealtimes

In our home, family meals have always been sacred. More than just food, they're a chance to connect. No matter how busy life got, dinner together remained a non-negotiable. When our children came along, we protected that tradition—and even now, with our sons mostly grown, we still savour every opportunity to share a meal, talk, laugh, and catch up as we linger at the dining table long after the last bit of food has been eaten. Sometimes our dinners are filled with laughter; other times, they're quiet and reflective. It doesn't matter. What matters is the togetherness. There's no need to force deep conversation—just let the moment unfold. Talk about the weather, faith, politics, or that hilarious reel from Instagram. It all counts.

Play Together

When the boys were younger, fun often meant spontaneity. We made up silly games in the car—counting yellow or red cars on the road—or kicked a football around the garden. Some of our games ended in laughter, others in fierce (and not always friendly!) competition. But we look back on all of it with fondness. One of us would often initiate a game, even when the other wasn't quite in the mood. But we tried to lean in—because we knew these moments were opportunities for connection. And more often than not, we ended up loving it. Now that our sons are grown, we don't get as many of those shared moments—but we still make the effort. Special occasions, casual hangouts—whatever it takes to keep the connection alive.

Make the Moments Count

It's not how many minutes we live that count, but the minutes we truly make count. So, seize every opportunity to create meaningful memories. Milestones like birthdays, anniversaries, graduations, and holidays are perfect opportunities to be intentional and make someone feel special. I still cherish the memory of our 20th wedding anniversary when Mary decided to mark it in a unique way— not with extravagant spending, but with heart. For 20 days leading up to the date, she posted one thing she admired about me each day on social media, each paired with a thoughtful photo. It made me feel seen and deeply valued—something I'll never forget. Now, as we celebrate our 30th anniversary by writing our first book and renewing our vows, we're once again choosing to create beautiful moments together.

But don't wait for big occasions—some of the most powerful memories come from everyday surprises. I love when Julius randomly posts a tribute about me online, just because. Even though he clarifies that it's not my birthday, people still flood the comments with birthday wishes! ☺ Just goes to show how busy life is. People are quick to like and comment, without even reading the post!

Be Intentional and Consistent

We both live very full lives— raising a family, running businesses, pastoring a church, organising community events, sometimes studying for exams—it all keeps our plates very full, but we've learned that if we don't make space for us, we risk losing what matters most. Modern life is overloaded with distractions. Technology was supposed to free us up, but it's only made us busier. If we're not intentional, we'll push aside our time together in favour of everything else. So, we guard our time fiercely. Yes, we sometimes fall behind. But we have a rule—when one of us says, *"Enough. It's time for us,"* we listen. We protect those moments the same way we'd protect a critical meeting or important deadline. Because they are that important.

Adapting and Evolving

Family life is fluid—it shifts and changes constantly. Our boys are grown now, and life looks very different from when we first started this journey. But even as seasons change, our commitment to each other remains our anchor. Now, we find ourselves back where we started—just the two of us. And instead of mourning what was, we're embracing what is. We're filling our lives with fresh traditions, shared activities, and meaningful moments that keep our relationship strong, joyful, and growing.

These moments—big and small—are your family's legacy. Not the houses, the titles, or the careers, but the memories made, the laughter shared, and the connection nurtured over time. So, protect them. Prioritise them. Celebrate them. Because in the end, it's not what you built that matters most—it's who you built it *with*.

Do Life Side by Side, Not Miles Apart—Application Steps

- ☑ **Plan to Ignite the Moment**—Take a moment to think about your next opportunity as a family to have a celebration. It could be a birthday, an anniversary, a child moving a grade up. How can you make it special. Remember, it's not about splashing out, but doing it with heart

- ☑ **Create a Shared Experience Jar**—Write down 15–20 simple, fun activities you'd love to do together—like trying a new recipe, going dancing, or exploring a new park. Place them in a jar and pull one out each week to enjoy. It's a great way to stay intentional and add an element of surprise to your quality time.

- ☑ **Start the "Check-In Over a Meal" Challenge**—for one week, share at least one daily meal without distractions. During the meal, each person shares a highlight, a lowlight, and something they're grateful for. These simple check-ins foster deeper conversations and create a rhythm of emotional connection in your everyday routine.

9

CULTIVATE A CULTURE OF MUTUAL RESPECT AND HONOUR

Speak To the Crown Not the Flaws

The way you speak to and treat your spouse helps shape how they see themselves—and ultimately, how they show up in the relationship. When you affirm their strengths and treat them with honour, you inspire them to rise to that identity. Criticism may correct momentarily, but honour transforms from the inside out.

Think about it—no one wants to feel disrespected, especially in their own home. Home should be your safe haven, a place where you feel seen, valued, and cherished. When life outside is tough and everything seems to be going wrong, walking through your front door should feel like entering an oasis—a place of peace, not pressure. But when disrespect creeps into the relationship, the home environment becomes emotionally unsafe, and the result is distance, tension, and disconnection.

Respect Isn't Earned—It's Given Freely

While respect cannot be demanded, don't wait for it to be earned either. It's tempting to think your spouse must earn your respect or honour through perfect behaviour, but the truth is, every human being—your spouse included—is inherently worthy of dignity. That worth is not based on performance; it's based on identity—they are God's highest creation, made in His image and for that alone, are worthy of respect. So rather than focus on their flaws, choose to speak to the crown within them. Speak to the potential, the greatness they carry, even if right now, it feels buried beneath poor behaviour, probably because of past hurt.

Everyone has a gem inside them, even if it's currently covered in dust. And here's the secret: the more you honour and affirm that gem, the more it begins to shine. This does not mean we don't correct, but constant criticism only hardens hearts and diminishes connection, while intentional words of honour water the seed of greatness inside your spouse. As Scripture reminds us, "God calls things that are not as though they were" [12]

The bible gives the account of Abraham, the Jewish Patriarch, whom God had promised would become the father of many nations, yet he was barren for several years without a single

---

[12] Romans 4:17

child. At some point, God changed his name from Abram, which meant *exalted father* in Hebrew, to Abraham, meaning *father of many nations*—long before he had a single child. That's the power of calling forth what's *possible*, not just describing what's *visible*. What names are you calling your spouse, perhaps not out loud, but in your heart? Lazy? Irresponsible? Clueless? Don't be surprised if they live up—or down—to your expectations. Your words carry power[13] and create atmosphere, identity, and ultimately, the trajectory of your relationship. They possess the ability to build up or tear down, to encourage or discourage. Honouring our spouse means consciously choosing kindness in our speech, affirming their worth, and diligently avoiding harsh, insensitive remarks, belittling comments, or dismissive language.

The Destructive Power of Disrespect

Disrespect isn't just about shouting or name-calling. It's in the subtle digs, dismissive tones, public put-downs, and unilateral decisions. Over time, dishonour eats away at trust and intimacy like rust on metal. A spouse who feels constantly disrespected may withdraw, become defensive, or even act out of pain. Dishonour doesn't just hurt feelings—it undermines the very foundation of your relationship. When you dishonour your spouse, you're not just tearing them down—you're damaging

---

[13] Proverbs 18:21

your own team. Remember, you are one. So, when one is diminished, the other suffers, whether it's immediately apparent on not.

Honour is a Lifestyle, Not an Occasional Gesture

Honour requires both humility and selflessness. It necessitates setting aside pride and ego, being willing to acknowledge our own imperfections, and recognizing the profound truth that our spouse's perspective is as valid as ours, and that sometimes they may even offer a wiser view. While the way we speak to our spouse is a strong indicator as to whether we honour them or not, true honour goes beyond polite manners. It is a lifestyle of consistently valuing your spouse's voice, needs, time, and presence. It's seen in how you make decisions, whether you value their opinion, and the way you treat them even when no one else is watching. It's also in how you think about them. Many people don't pay enough attention to their thoughts. Again, our favourite book in the whole world, the Bible, tells us that out of the abundance of the heart, the mouth speaks.[14] This means your words are only a reflection of your thoughts. If you don't honour your spouse in your heart, it's only a matter of time before it shows in your words and your actions.

---

[14] Matthew 12:34

Here are a few practical ways to show respect and honour to your spouse:

- **Value their opinion:** Don't make major decisions without their input. Even if you think you "know best," respect the process of unity. Let your spouse feel heard.

- **Mind your language:** Watch your tone. Speak kindly and avoid sarcasm or words that belittle.

- **Celebrate their efforts:** Say "thank you" often—even for things that happen every day like cooking, helping with the kids, or running errands.

- **Make them feel valued:** Avoid interrupting or dismissing their thoughts during conversations.

- **Make them feel safe:** Cultivate emotional and psychological safety in your home. Be someone they can trust with their vulnerability.

- **Don't correct or criticise in public:** This creates shame and disconnection. Honour protects.

- **Practice active listening:** Show genuine interest in what they're saying.

- **Be thoughtful with your actions:** Little gestures of kindness— like making their tea, running a bath, or a loving note—can speak volumes.

- **Apologise when you're wrong:** It shows humility and builds trust.

- **Affirm them before others:** Speak well of them even when they're not around. Let your words affirm their character and worth, not diminish it.

Mirror the Standard You Desire

What if your spouse isn't acting honourably? What if your respect isn't being reciprocated?

It can be difficult, when your daily experience and their actions are a far cry from that of royalty, but we encourage you to walk by faith, not by sight.[15] Start with you. Be the change you want to see. You don't have to wait to be treated like royalty before you treat your spouse like royalty. Lead by example. When you elevate your spouse, you elevate your relationship. The seeds you plant today in honour will bear fruit tomorrow, even if you don't see immediate change. Is it easy to keep honouring someone that dishonours you or to keep respecting something that disrespects you? —certainly not! But remember, honour is not just about what they deserve—it's about who you choose to be. When you consistently model respect, you invite transformation, not just in your spouse, but in your marriage. You create a standard of love that rises above temporary

---

[15] 2 Corinthians 5:7

challenges. We did say the bible has the final say in our lives and marriage and the bible teaches *"be devoted to one another in love. Honor one another above yourselves."* [16] We embrace this principle and try to live it out daily and it has helped us cultivate a culture of honour in our home.

The Overflow of Respect

Mutual respect naturally leads to heartfelt appreciation—not just for grand gestures, but even in the little things. Acknowledge each other's efforts. Say thank you for the ordinary. Take nothing for granted. Honestly, we're guilty of this more than we'd like to admit. It's easy to overlook the everyday things—laundry, meals, tidying up—because they feel routine. But those small acts are acts of love, and they deserve recognition.

Creating a culture of honour won't happen overnight. It takes time, intention, and sometimes uncomfortable self-awareness. But it's worth it. Start small. Even if you stumble, keep going. You don't need to be perfect—you just need to be consistent. Start by asking yourself some tough questions and be brutally honest with yourself.

How would you describe the current culture of honour and respect in your relationship? Is it something you're

---

[16] Romans 12:10

cultivating intentionally or something you've allowed to form on its own?

What thoughts have you been thinking about your spouse and what words have you been speaking to, or about them lately? Are they words that affirm their value and potential— or ones that only criticize and point out flaws?

Do you find it easy or difficult to appreciate your spouse for the "everyday" things? Why? What stops you from expressing more gratitude?

Your home can be the oasis you both long for. A place of refuge, not ridicule. A space where you both flourish, feel safe, and feel seen. When honour becomes the atmosphere of your marriage, your relationship won't just survive—it will thrive.

Cultivate a Culture of Mutual Respect and Honour—Application Steps

☑ **Take Stock of Your Tone**—Be deliberate in how you speak, especially when you're frustrated or angry. Pause, breathe, slow down and pick your words carefully. Raising your voice at someone does not communicate honour and respect.

☑ **Seek out their opinion**—Ask your spouse's opinion on a decision you'd normally make on your own—then really listen and consider their input.

☑ **Express Your Admiration**—Pick one or two things you admire or appreciate about your spouse and tell them—if you can't think of anything, it means they have been overlooked. Look again!

10

EXPRESS APPRECIATION AND GRATITUDE

Not Taking Each Other For Granted

As a trained solicitor, one of the principles Mary learned in university—one that has stayed with her ever since—is this: *"Equity must not only be done but must be seen to be done."* This principle emphasizes the importance of not just doing the right thing, but ensuring it is evident to all that the right thing has been done. In many ways, this applies directly to relationships, particularly marriage.

In marriage, it is easy to assume that love and appreciation are understood without being expressed. We tend to believe that because we love and appreciate our spouse, they automatically know it. But the truth is, unspoken appreciation is often unfelt appreciation. No one is a mind reader. If you don't express your love and gratitude, your spouse may not fully realize how much they mean to you.

Ironically, those we cherish the most are often the ones we take most for granted. We may be intentional about showing kindness and appreciation to colleagues, friends, or even strangers, yet when it comes to our spouse—the one we have committed to love and honour for life—we sometimes assume they "just know" how we feel. We invest effort in other relationships but can become complacent in the one that matters most. But love and appreciation must be *demonstrated*. It is not enough to assume that your spouse knows how grateful you are for them and how much you appreciate them. They need to hear it, see it, and feel it. A heartfelt "thank you" or a thoughtful act of appreciation can make all the difference in making your spouse feel valued.

The Danger in Taking Each Other for Granted

Failing to express appreciation can create emotional distance over time. At first, your spouse may brush it off. But as the pattern continues, resentment can start to build, which could even start to be expressed as anger. You might find your spouse often gets angry for no apparent reason. When someone repeatedly feels unappreciated and undervalued, they may begin to question their importance in the relationship. Over time, they might withdraw, stop putting in as much effort, or even look for validation elsewhere. This is especially true for spouses who are naturally inclined to "just get on with it." Those who don't frequently voice their needs may not complain, but that does not mean they don't *feel* the effects of being taken for granted. Even the most independent and self-sufficient person still desires to feel valued.

Understanding Differences in the Need for Appreciation

Everyone loves to feel appreciated, but the degree to which people *need* that appreciation varies. Factors like personality, upbringing, and life experiences influence how individuals express and receive gratitude. One of the most transformative experiences in our relationship—second only to the impact of God's word—was taking the Maxwell DISC assessment and receiving our DISC Reports. It was truly a game-changer. Leveraging her expertise as a certified Human Behaviour Specialist and DISC Consultant, Mary was able to break down the insights in our reports, helping us understand ourselves and each other on a much deeper level.

Our reports showed that Julius is an **IS** on the DISC spectrum, meaning he is highly people-oriented and thrives on verbal affirmation and appreciation. Mary on the other hand, is a **DC**, which means she is highly task-oriented and focused on efficiency. This fundamental difference in our personalities had a significant impact on how we related to one another.

For Julius, words of affirmation and appreciation are deeply meaningful. He thrives when his efforts are acknowledged and valued. Mary's natural inclination on the other hand is to focus on *what still needs to be done* rather than stopping to celebrate what has already been accomplished. Her tendency is to walk into a room and immediately notice what is *wrong* or incomplete rather than appreciating what has already been done. Not because she is ungrateful, but because her mind is wired to constantly move on to the next task.

You can imagine how this dynamic played out in our marriage. While Julius craved appreciation for his efforts, I was often too focused on moving on to the next thing to pause and acknowledge his contributions. Reading each other's DISC Reports gave us a deeper understanding of how we're wired and what truly motivates us. We realized that neither of us was being petty nor making a big deal out of nothing when we craved more of what naturally fuels us—it was simply a reflection of our individual needs.

Now, I make a more conscious effort to express appreciation to Julius and say "well done" more often—even if I sometimes follow it up with what still needs to be done! 😊 And in turn, I don't get as frustrated as I used to when Mary seems to overlook what has been done, focusing instead on what still needs attention. 😊

Overcoming the Barriers to Showing Appreciation

Several factors can prevent spouses from actively showing appreciation:

Busyness and Routine: Life gets busy, and routines take over. It's easy to overlook appreciation when you're juggling so many responsibilities.

Different Expectations: Some people were raised in homes where verbal affirmation wasn't common, so they may not realize the importance of expressing appreciation in marriage.

Personality Differences: As mentioned earlier, some people naturally express appreciation more readily than others. If this is not something that comes naturally to you, and not one of your motivators, you might not readily appreciate its importance.

Unresolved Hurt or Resentment: If past conflicts haven't been properly addressed, it can be hard to express gratitude freely.

Whatever barriers you may be experiencing in your own relationship, the good news is that they *can* be overcome. It just takes intentionality. While we don't do what we do for our spouses or family just so that we can receive thanks and accolade, it does feel good when what one does is recognised and appreciated.

Appreciating each other's efforts strengthens your bond. It creates a marriage where both spouses feel seen, valued, and cherished. When gratitude becomes a natural part of your relationship, it fosters warmth, mutual respect, and deeper emotional connection. No matter how long you've been married, it's never too late to start showing appreciation. The more you practice it, the more it becomes second nature, and the more fulfilling your marriage will be. Don't wait for a special occasion—start today!

Express Appreciation and Gratitude—Application Steps

☑ **Say It Often**—Make a decision to verbally appreciate your spouse daily, whether for something they did or simply for who they are. A simple "Thank you for all you do" or "I really appreciate the way you handled that" can mean a lot.

☑ **Show It Through Actions**—Action still speaks louder than words. As often as you can manage it, go out of your way to *do something special* for your spouse. You could cook their favourite meal, give a thoughtful gift, send them a handwritten letter. It does not have to be grand or expensive. It just needs to be thoughtful, that's what will make it special.

☑ **Have Regular Gratitude Parties**—Turn it into a special date night—order your favourite takeout, share a bottle of wine, and shower each other with words of appreciation. This intentional practice will help you reflect on and acknowledge the things you may often take for granted in each other.

☑ **Be Intentional**—Expressing gratitude often requires intentional effort, especially if it doesn't come naturally. Setting a reminder doesn't mean there's a problem in your marriage—it's simply a way to prioritize what matters. Life gets busy, and what isn't scheduled often gets overlooked!

11

CELEBRATE YOUR INDIVIDUAL UNIQUENESS

Treasuring the Value Each Party Brings to the Union

"Two are better than one because they get a good reward for their labour."[17] This ancient wisdom has been a living truth in our marriage. A strong, thriving union isn't just about co-existing under one roof or bearing the same last name—it's about intentionally combining our distinct identities, strengths, and perspectives to create something stronger and more beautiful than we could have imagined. At the heart of our union lies a strong and deliberate acknowledgement and appreciation of the unique value we each bring to our home. But that wasn't always the case.

In the early days, we both came into the relationship with strong personalities and big dreams. Naturally, that meant we clashed— often. We both had our way of seeing the world, our

---

[17] Ecclesiastes 4:9-12

way of doing things, and our way of responding to challenges. And if we're honest, we each believed our way was the better way. Like many couples, we initially saw our differences as threats rather than gifts. Instead of embracing each other's uniqueness, we tried (consciously or not) to reshape one another. If only the other person could think like me, process like me, or respond like me—things would be smoother, right? But with time, patience, and a growing understanding, we began to see that our differences weren't obstacles; they were actually tools—different but equally essential. They were strengths meant to complement each other, not compete.

When Differences Create Tension

Take, for example, decision-making. One party may be naturally methodical—prefers to think things through, consider every angle, make lists, and weigh the risks. The other might be a visionary— driven by intuition, quick decisions, and bold leaps. You can see how this difference could lead to frustration: "Why don't you slow down and think this through?" would clash with "Why are you overthinking everything?" Take a closer look however, and you will see the beauty in both approaches. One brings caution; the other brings courage. Together, they can make wiser, bolder choices than they could alone.

It might be that in your home, one party is the organized planner, while the other brings spontaneity and fun. One might be incredibly detail-oriented, while the other prefers to stay in the big picture. These differences, when appreciated, become the ingredients for a dynamic and well-rounded partnership. When misunderstood, though, they can lead to power struggles and frustration.

From Clashing to Collaborating

Our journey has taught us that the key isn't sameness—it's synergy. It's about choosing to see our spouse through a lens of gratitude rather than frustration. It's recognising that their way, though different, has value and brings value. We've come to treasure the individual flair each of us bring to our home. The quirks, the perspectives, the problem-solving styles, the gifts—it's all part of the masterpiece we're creating together. Instead of striving for 50/50, we both show up 100%. Fully present. Fully ourselves. Fully invested.

This approach has helped us avoid the trap of scorekeeping. Instead of "I did this, so you should do that," we think in terms of we. We are on the same team. We're both building, both giving, both showing up fully to this shared mission called marriage. Think about it: What unique strengths does your spouse bring into the relationship that you might have overlooked or misunderstood in the past? Are there areas where you've tried to change your spouse instead of embracing their uniqueness? How has that impacted your relationship?

When you start to treasure the value your spouse brings—even if it's wildly different from how you'd do things—your marriage becomes a space where both of you can thrive. You both feel celebrated and safe to bring your whole selves to the table.

Celebrate Your Individual Uniqueness— Application Steps

☑ **Strength Swap**—Each of you should write down three strengths you see in the other. Then take turns sharing why you admire those traits—and how they've positively impacted your marriage.

☑ **Team Time**—Next time a decision needs to be made, try approaching it from each other's perspective first. Let the "planner" lead the risk analysis, and the "visionary" paint the big picture. Then come together to decide.

☑ **Shift the Energy**—When next you find yourself feeling frustrated because of your spouse's different approach, attitude or perspective. Catch yourself and immediately shift the energy. Ask yourself what strength they are exhibiting that you might be overlooking because you are stuck in your way and celebrate that instead.

12

INCREASE YOUR VALUE

Investing in Yourself to Be an Asset, not a Liability

Amarriage where one person gives, while the other simply takes is not sustainable. Imagine a business where one partner is constantly investing time, effort, and resources while the other partner does nothing to improve the company's prospects. Sooner or later, the contributing partner will feel drained and undervalued, and the partnership will struggle to survive. In the same way, if only one spouse bears the responsibility of enriching the relationship, it will eventually feel lopsided. Marriage is about mutual support and shared effort. It is a team effort where both partners should seek to grow and contribute in meaningful ways.

A thriving marriage is built on partnership, and every partnership is only as strong as the individuals in it. When both partners are growing, evolving, and bringing more value to the relationship, the marriage flourishes. But when one partner is stagnant—whether financially, intellectually, emotionally, or spiritually—it creates an imbalance. The weight of responsibilities begins to rest too heavily on one person, and over time, resentment and frustration can creep in.

When we met, Julius was a cab driver. He was hardworking, responsible, and independent. He had a rented flat and was one of the very few people in our church who owned a car. ☺ From his perspective, he was doing quite well. However, I challenged him by asking what his aspirations were—what he was working toward, what his plans were for the future. He later admitted that my question caught him off guard because, at the time, he felt there was nothing more to aspire to. But that simple question sparked a shift in his mindset. It made him think beyond his current comfort zone and begin to envision greater possibilities for his life.

In the same vein, when we met, Mary shared with me, her dream of one day running her own law firm. I didn't just listen—I encouraged her. I kept reminding her of her goal, challenging her not to settle, pushing her to take steps toward making it a reality. That encouragement and accountability played a huge role in her eventually setting up her own law firm in 2005.

To this day, we continue to challenge each other to grow, develop, and become the best versions of ourselves. And this is the key to a strong marriage: both partners committing to continued growth and development, continually investing in themselves, not just for themselves, but for the sake of the relationship.

But what exactly does it mean to invest in yourself? Growth can happen in many ways. Here we touch on four.

Four Key Arears to Increase Your Value

1. Elevate Your Mindset

Your mind is one of your greatest assets, and the way you think shapes your entire life—including your marriage. A sharp, well-informed, and ever-evolving mindset brings depth to a relationship because it broadens your perspective, and perspective is key. Our perspective, while not always the absolute truth, becomes our truth, and influences how we interpret and respond to everything around us.

Imagine wearing blue-tinted glasses. No matter how much someone insists that the world is not blue, you won't believe them because *blue* is all you see. In the same way, our mindset acts as a lens through which we view life. If we have a limited or negative perspective, it distorts reality and affects how we engage with our spouse and the world around us. But when we invest in our personal growth and allow new insights to reshape our thinking, we gain a richer, fuller understanding of life—enhancing not only our own experience but also our relationships.

Many people stop actively learning after finishing school, but the most successful and fulfilled individuals commit to lifelong learning. This doesn't necessarily mean pursuing formal education—though that can be valuable. It simply means continuously expanding your knowledge in ways that refine and elevate your thinking.

We are the direct products of our thoughts. The quality of our lives is determined by the quality of our thinking because, ultimately, *we become what we think*. When you expand your mindset, you enhance your ability to process challenges, navigate relationships, and make better decisions. Higher-quality thoughts lead to a higher-quality life—affecting your marriage, career, and personal fulfilment in ways you never imagined.

2. Enhance Your Inter-personal Skills

Theodore Roosevelt once said, *"The most important single ingredient in the formula of success is knowing how to get along with people."* People are at the heart of everything we do—we cannot succeed in life without people. It is very easy to think that because we interact with others every day, we must be naturally good at it, but this is not true. Strong interpersonal skills does come automatically; it must be intentionally developed, but it is so well worth the investment if we want to build meaningful, enriching relationships.

John D. Rockefeller, one of the most successful businessmen in history, famously stated, *"I will pay more for the ability to deal with people than for any other under the sun."* Given that he was worth $1.4 billion at the time of his death in 1937, it's safe to say he understood the value of investing in the right skills, and few skills are as valuable in life as the ability to communicate effectively, navigate emotions, and relate well with others. Developing strong interpersonal skills requires a commitment to raising self-awareness, effective communication, and emotional intelligence—three crucial yet often overlooked elements of a thriving relationship.

Self-Awareness: If you lack self-awareness, you will struggle with internal conflicts, not understanding why you act how you act or why you respond to certain things the way you do.

Effective Communication: One of our favourite quotes is one by George Bernard Shaw which states, *"The single biggest problem in communication is the illusion that it has taken place."* Just because we talk to each other every day doesn't mean we are communicating well. Good communication requires active listening, understanding tone and body language, and learning how to express yourself clearly and respectfully. Effective communication in most cases does not come naturally. It is a skill that needs to be cultivated and developed. We share more on this in a subsequent chapter.

Emotional Intelligence: As mentioned in a previous chapter, if one partner lacks emotional intelligence, the marriage can quickly become unstable and strained.

Some people might say, *"I'm just not a people person,"* or *"I struggle to express myself."* But interpersonal skills, like any other skill, can be learned and refined. Investing in this area will not only improve your marriage but also make you a better listener, a more empathetic partner, and a more emotionally secure individual. You'll learn to manage emotions rather than reacting impulsively. Instead of lashing out in anger, shutting down during conflicts, or engaging in other harmful behaviours that hinder communication and damage intimacy, you'll develop the ability to navigate challenges with patience and understanding.

3. Increase Your Financial Value

Money is one of the biggest sources of stress in marriage. When one partner carries the financial burden while the other makes little or no effort to contribute or grow financially, frustration and resentment can build over time. This is why investing in yourself to increase your financial value is crucial—not just for your personal growth but for the well-being of your marriage and family. That said, there is no *one-size-fits-all* approach. The financial dynamics of a marriage depends on the couple's vision for their family, their financial goals, and the values they both agree on. This is such an important topic; we delve deeper in chapter 10.

4. Take Responsibility in the Home

A strong marriage is built on shared responsibilities. When one person feels like they are carrying the weight of the household— whether in raising children, managing the home, or making all major decisions—it inevitably leads to exhaustion and frustration. A marriage thrives when both partners are invested in the home and family life, not just in their designated roles but in ways that ensure neither party feels overwhelmed, nor taken for granted.

That said, again, we appreciate that every family dynamic is different, and what works for one couple may not work for another. However, even in cases for example where the couples have agreed that one partner will be the primary breadwinner while the other takes on the bulk of household and childcare responsibilities, it's still important that the breadwinning spouse does not completely detach from home life.

If there are children involved, both parents must be active participants in their upbringing for the sake of their emotional and mental well-being. A child's healthy development requires love, guidance, and involvement from BOTH parents. It is not in the best interest of a child for one parent to be absent from their daily lives, major milestones, and key decisions simply because they are focused on work.

Here are some ways both partners can take responsibility in the home to strengthen their marriage and family life:

Be proactive in sharing household duties: Instead of waiting to be asked, take the initiative in managing household responsibilities. Whether it's cooking, cleaning, grocery shopping, or handling repairs, both partners should contribute in ways that ease the load for each other. In our home, for example—thanks to Julius—we established a cooking rota, ensuring that everyone, including our adult children when they're home, take turns in the kitchen. Had Julius not insisted on this system (and on getting the boys involved), I would have likely continued cooking seven days a week, simply because of my "just get on with it" mindset.

Admittedly, at first, I was tempted to take over to avoid the inevitable mess and the food not tasting quite how I wanted it. 😊 But over time, both the boys' cooking skills and their tidiness improved. Now, on the rare occasions when I end up cooking more than my share, I grumble—and Julius is quick to remind me that if not for him, I'd still be in the kitchen every night!

Share your parenting responsibility. If one spouse handles most of the parenting tasks, the other should step up to balance the load. This could mean assisting with homework, attending school events, disciplining when necessary, or simply spending intentional quality time with the children. No one parent should ever feel like a single parent in a two-parent home.

Make decisions together: While one partner may naturally take the lead in certain areas, major decisions—whether about finances, parenting, career moves, or household management—should be made as a team. While both spouses may not always be directly involved in executing every plan, the key is to ensure that decisions are discussed and agreed upon together. A strong marriage operates with a shared vision, and when one person is left to make all the key decisions alone, it can create an imbalance in the relationship, leaving the other feeling unheard or disconnected from the family's direction. Over time, this lack of collaboration can lead to division and, in some cases, even set the stage for "grey divorce" later in life, when long-standing disconnection finally takes its toll.

Taking responsibility in the home is not necessarily about rigid roles; it's about ensuring both partners feel valued, supported, and engaged in your shared life. It's about being reliable and carrying your own share of the family's responsibilities. If for example, you keep 'forgetting' to do what you said you would do, and keep dropping the ball, causing your spouse to be inconvenienced and sometimes resulting in loss to the family, it could weaken your union. A thriving marriage is one where both individuals are equally committed to making their home a place of love, stability, and mutual dependence.

The Mindset Shift: From Burden to Blessing

To truly add value to your marriage, shift your mindset from *"What can I get?"* to *"What can I give?"* Instead of relying on your spouse to carry the weight, strive to grow into someone who enriches their life. A strong, fulfilling marriage is built on two whole, evolving individuals. When one partner refuses to grow—emotionally, intellectually, spiritually, or financially—it creates an imbalance. But when both are intentional about self-improvement, they build a resilient, thriving partnership that stands the test of time.

We are both committed to lifelong learning, constantly investing in our personal and professional growth. Julius actively pursues certifications and qualifications to stay competitive in the IT marketplace, and Mary continues to enhance her expertise in training and development. By doing so, we've not only increased our earning potential but have also remained intellectually aligned. This has been invaluable in strengthening our relationship, minimizing discord, and ensuring we continue to share a common perspective on life's choices, big or small.

So, invest in yourself. Read books, listen to podcasts, take courses—pay for them if necessary—you and your spouse are worth the investment!

Increase Your Value—Application Steps

☑ **Elevate Your Mindset**—Choose one area in which you need to change your mindset and set a goal to do something every day that will help you grow in that area. It could be reading a book, taking an online course, listening to a podcast or doing something that takes you out of your comfort zone.

☑ **Enhance Your Interpersonal Skills**—Practice active listening in your daily conversations. Make a conscious effort to listen more than you speak, ask clarifying questions, and respond with empathy, paying attention to your tone, body language, and facial expressions to ensure your communication fosters connection rather than conflict.

☑ **Increase Your Financial Value**—Do you have a financial goal for the next 12 months? If not, sit down with your partner and create one, then together come up with a plan on how the goal will be achieved. Things don't always go as planned, but plans are great starting points. If you fail to plan, you may just be planning to fail!

☑ **Take Responsibility in the Home**—Identify one household or parenting responsibility that your partner primarily handles and make a commitment to contribute more. Whether it's planning meals, helping with homework, or managing household finances.

13

EMBRACE GOOD MONEY MANAGEMENT

Financial Unity Through Good Stewardship and Accountability

As mentioned in a previous chapter, there is no one-size-fits-all approach to managing finances in marriage. Every couple's financial dynamic depends on their vision for their family, their goals, and the values they both agree on. Some couples may decide that one spouse will be the sole breadwinner while the other focuses on raising the children and managing the home. If this is a shared decision that aligns with their goals and expectations, it can work beautifully.

Problems arise when partners have differing values and expectations about financial contributions and resource management. For instance, if one spouse makes no financial contribution to the family or manages money poorly—often due to their own personal expectations or upbringing—especially when the household income is insufficient to meet the family's needs—it creates tension and conflict. The burden of carrying the entire financial load falls unfairly on one partner, leading to feelings of resentment and frustration. Mary often jokingly says "What's mine is mine, and what's yours is mine," but unfortunately, some people genuinely adopt this mindset when it comes to family finances. This attitude, however, only breeds discord and ultimately harms the relationship.

This does not mean both parties must earn the same amount of money, but it does mean that each spouse should take responsibility for their own financial growth. Whether through further education, career advancement, or starting a side business, each partner in the marriage partnership should be thinking about how they can enhance their financial value to support their family's financial goals.

True financial value is however not just about earning more but about making responsible financial decisions that contribute to the long-term security and well-being of the family. Financial value includes financial literacy—learning to manage money wisely, budgeting effectively, and making smart investments for the future. A financially responsible and forward-thinking spouse adds stability to the marriage, while poor money management and financial recklessness can create unnecessary stress and discord.

It is worth pointing out that financial strain is one of the leading causes of divorce. Poor money management, hidden debts, and mismatched financial priorities can create deep divisions in a marriage. If one partner prioritizes 'keeping up with the Joneses' over building financial stability, constantly overspending, maxing out credit cards, and taking on debt to fund a lavish lifestyle that drains rather than strengthens the family, serious financial strain will follow. Over time, this kind of financial recklessness can erode trust, create resentment, and even threaten the stability of the relationship. When both partners however are aligned in their financial mindset and work together toward shared goals, they create a foundation of stability that strengthens both their marriage and their future

Understanding Financial Unity

Remember the goal in marriage is oneness, becoming one in every aspect of life—emotionally, spiritually, physically, and financially.

Financial unity means seeing money not as "his" or "hers" but as "ours." It's about moving from a mindset of individual ownership to joint stewardship. As already mentioned, this does not mean both spouses must earn the same amount, but it does mean that each contribute—whether financially or by managing household responsibilities—and that they work toward common financial goals together. Decisions about significant expenses, investments, and long-term financial plans should be made together. This enables both partners to develop a sense of ownership and responsibility toward the family's financial future.

It's important to understand that true financial unity does not necessarily mean holding joint bank accounts or joint assets. While joint accounts can be helpful, they won't prevent financial conflict if one partner frequently makes unapproved purchases, overspends causing the account to become overdrawn or has a spending habit that is at odds with the family's financial goals. True financial unity is about recognizing that everything you both own belongs to both of you, being responsible stewards of the resources God has entrusted to you, aligning your financial decisions with shared goals, and maintaining accountability to one another.

Financial unity thrives on openness. Being transparent about income, expenses, debts, and future goals ensures that both spouses are on the same page. When you get married, the concept of "my money" and "your money" should be replaced with "our money." This shift in mindset builds trust and promotes transparency. In our experience, it's not uncommon for people to be warned by their parents or others—often due to negative experiences in their own marriages—against being completely open about finances.

While this advice may be well-intentioned, it can actually do more harm than good. If financial transparency is practiced from the beginning, it eliminates suspicion and cultivates security. Keeping separate accounts, secret spending or hiding financial decisions from one another only creates unnecessary barriers and breeds distrust. You have to make a choice: will you allow someone else's experience to shape your reality, or will you chart your own course? As we've pointed out in previous chapters, honesty, vulnerability, and transparency may feel risky, but they are risks worth taking to build the strong, unified marriage you desire.

When both partners are intentional about practicing financial unity, they experience not only greater financial stability but also deeper emotional and spiritual connection. Money no longer becomes a source of division but a tool for building a thriving, God-honouring marriage where both spouses feel secure, valued, and united.

Embrace Good Money Management—Application Steps

☑ **Create a Budget and Financial Plan Together**—Create a unified budget that reflects your shared financial values and priorities. Identify your essential expenses, allocate funds for savings, and set limits on discretionary spending. A budget serves as a guide to keep you both accountable and moving toward your long-term goals

☑ **Have Regular Money Conversations**—Set aside time regularly— whether weekly, monthly or quarterly—to discuss your finances openly. Review your income, expenses, savings, and future goals together. Use this time to assess progress toward shared financial goals and address any concerns before they become bigger issues. Transparency in these conversations builds trust and helps both partners stay aligned.

☑ **Agree on Boundaries for Large Spending**—Decide in advance what constitutes "major spending" and agree on a threshold amount that requires mutual approval. This practice ensures that both spouses feel involved in significant financial decisions and prevents misunderstandings or resentment about unapproved spending. It reinforces the principle of shared stewardship and mutual respect.

☑ **Seek Wise Counsel When Needed**—There is safety in a multitude of counsellors provided they are the right counsellors.[18] When financial challenges feel overwhelming, seek guidance from trusted mentors, financial advisors, counsellors or coaches who can provide objective and biblically grounded advice to help you get unstuck and moving forward.

---

[18] Proverbs 11:14

14

ADOPT A 'NO SECRETS, NO BARRIERS' STANCE

Embracing Complete Honesty, Transparency, and Vulnerability

Depending on your past experiences—or even the experiences of others you've observed—you may enter marriage cautiously, holding back in some areas in an attempt to protect yourself in the event things don't work out. On the surface, this might seem like a wise strategy, but in reality, it sets your marriage up for failure.

Marriage was never designed to be a cautious, half-hearted commitment. The biblical vision for marriage—which is what we wholeheartedly adhere to—is one of complete unity. A bond so deep that two individuals become one.[19] This unity is not just physical; it encompasses emotional, spiritual, and relational oneness. It doesn't mean you lose your individuality or personal identity, but it does mean that your lives become deeply intertwined.

---

[19] Genesis 2:24

In our relationship, we both have our personal spaces, yet there is no space—physical or emotional—where the other is not welcome. There are no locked doors, no secret compartments, no hidden corners. When you truly embrace this level of unity, you are no longer two separate people navigating life independently but a united front, deeply connected in every way.

The Damage of Dishonesty

If trust is the foundation of a strong marriage, dishonesty is the wrecking ball that can bring it all crashing down. The moment deceit enters a relationship, whether through small white lies or significant betrayals, it plants seeds of doubt that can quickly grow into a deep chasm of distrust.

Julius often recounts an encounter he once had with a man who was drunk at the time but offered him incredibly valuable advice. The man said to him "never, ever be unfaithful to your wife. I made the mistake of being unfaithful to my wife once, and even though she has forgiven me, and we are still together, every once in a while, she reminds me" Trust once broken, can be incredibly difficult to rebuild. Even if forgiveness is granted, there will always be lingering questions of doubt and uncertainties.

Never lie, not to your spouse or anyone else—it's simply not worth it! As we have already mentioned, our faith plays an extremely important role in every aspect of our lives. For us, living by biblical principles isn't just about us and the benefits to us. it's about our love, reverence, commitment, and submission to God's word, and the Bible is clear about the importance of truthfulness. In fact, it tells us that God detests lying lips, but He delights in those who tell the truth.[20] As we surrender our lives to God and choose to walk in His truth, we naturally reap the benefits of a marriage built on integrity, trust, and lasting unity, and enjoy security that honesty brings to our marriage.

So, lying, in any form, should be a no-go in marriage—period. Even when we think we are protecting our spouse from pain, dishonesty only makes things worse in the long run. Ask yourself, *"What will be the consequences when the truth eventually comes out?"* Because the truth almost always does come out. And when it does, the pain of betrayal is often far worse than whatever discomfort the truth might have initially caused.

Another thing to consider is that if your spouse knows you lie to others, it's only a matter of time before they start wondering if you are lying to them as well. A spouse who regularly deceives others— whether in small things like making excuses to avoid commitments or bigger issues like financial dishonesty—plants seeds of doubt in their marriage. Trust isn't just about believing what your spouse tells you; it's about believing in their integrity as a person. Even if you are not ready

---

[20] Proverbs 12:22

to share something deeply personal, it's better to say, *"I'm not ready to talk about that right now,"* than to lie. Honesty, even when difficult, builds trust. Dishonesty, even when well-intended, erodes it.

Sometimes the truth stings, but we owe it to our spouse to speak it in love. If we believe they're wrong about something, we say so—not to criticize, but to protect them from believing a lie. After all, if we don't tell them, who will? This also extends to how we relate to others. We don't automatically take each other's side in every situation. Instead, we're committed to truth—even when it means acknowledging that one of us was wrong. That kind of integrity builds trust, strengthens accountability, and keeps our relationship rooted in reality, not illusion.

Challenges to Complete Honesty, Transparency and Vulnerability

Even with the best intentions, many people struggle to be completely open in relationships and while one could attribute several reasons to that, we believe a major overarching reason people hold back from being completely honest, transparent and vulnerable in relationships is FEAR. They may have a fear of their spouse's reaction should they reveal their struggles, concerns, insecurities, or mistakes, or fear that it could lead to an unpleasant outcome. Let's look at some common fears that could hinder honesty, transparency and vulnerability in relationships:

Fear of Being Judged: This fear often stems from past experiences where perhaps being honest led to criticism, rejection, or ridicule. As a result, we may develop a habit of concealing our true selves, presenting only the parts that seem safe and acceptable to avoid being judged or labelled in a certain way.

Fear of Rejection: Closely tied to the fear of judgment is the fear of rejection. If you're afraid that being completely honest and transparent about who you are or expressing your true thoughts and feelings might lead your spouse to withdraw their love or acceptance, you will naturally hold back. Likewise, if you're unsure whether your displays of love, affection, and vulnerability will be reciprocated, the fear of having that love rejected can cause you to withhold it. This emotional guardedness creates distance and prevents the deep connection that true intimacy requires.

Fear of Being Misunderstood: The fear of being misunderstood can lead you to withhold parts of yourself, avoiding deep or difficult conversations to prevent misinterpretation of your words, intentions, or emotions. When you worry that expressing your true feelings may be taken the wrong way or create unnecessary conflict, you may choose silence over honesty. However, this avoidance often results in emotional distance and missed opportunities for genuine connection, as true intimacy thrives when both partners feel heard and understood.

Fear of Being Taken Advantage of

The fear of being taken advantage of can create emotional barriers, causing guarded communication and a reluctance to fully invest in the relationship. This fear is often rooted in past experiences of betrayal or emotional wounds, where trust was broken, leaving scars that make it difficult to be vulnerable again. As a result, one may withhold affection, support, or openness, fearing that giving too much might lead to being exploited or unappreciated. However, maintaining these walls can prevent true intimacy and hinder the growth of a healthy, mutually fulfilling relationship.

Fear of Conflict: Some people hate conflict and will avoid it at all costs and so may avoid expressing their true thoughts or feelings to prevent arguments or tension. This often leads to bottling up emotions or agreeing outwardly while harbouring unspoken frustrations, which will only gradually erode trust and intimacy. While avoiding conflict may seem like keeping the peace, unresolved issues can build up over time, creating distance and resentment. True connection thrives when both partners feel safe enough to address difficult conversations with love and respect.

Fear of Disappointment: If you think that your spouse might not respond in the way you hope when you express how you feel and your true needs or emotions, you may just hold back from expressing them. No one likes the unpleasant feeling of disappointment and so rather than risk feeling hurt or invalidated, we convince ourselves we and the relationship are better off if we keep our feelings, desires and expectations to ourselves. But this is self-sabotaging, as over time, this reluctance to open up can create emotional distance damaging us and the relationship we are trying to protect.

Fear of Burdening Your Spouse: Another reason some people may hold back from being completely honest, transparent and vulnerable is the concern that it will put too much emotional weight on their partner. Out of a desire to protect your spouse from stress or worry, you may hesitate to share their own struggles, weaknesses, desires, or emotional pain believing it's better to carry the burden alone. While this intention may come from a place of love and care, it can lead to emotional isolation, preventing you from experiencing the deep connection that comes from supporting one another through life's challenges.

Overcoming Challenges to Complete Honesty, Transparency, and Vulnerability

Fear can be paralyzing. It prevents action and leads to building walls intended for protection, but these same walls often become prisons that keep you isolated. Since the ultimate goal of marriage is complete oneness, we must be intentional about removing anything that hinders this unity. Dishonesty, lack of transparency, and fear of vulnerability build barriers instead of bridges, making true connection impossible.

The Bible gives us a glimpse of God's original design for marriage: *"And they were both naked, the man and his wife, and were not ashamed."*[21] This nakedness was not just physical—it was emotional and spiritual as well. It reflects a state of complete transparency where neither partner feared shame or rejection. A healthy marriage should create that same safe space where both spouses can be fully known and fully loved. When grace and unconditional love are extended, honesty, openness, and vulnerability become far less intimidating.

If you've been keeping a back door open in your marriage— an emotional escape plan in case things don't work out—it's time to shut that door and throw yourself wholeheartedly into the relationship. Leaving an exit strategy in place is a recipe for disaster because, eventually, you'll take it. True intimacy can only be built when both partners commit fully, without reservations or conditions.

In our relationship, we have chosen to know everything about each other's lives. There are no hidden passwords, no off-limits

---

[21] Genesis 2:25

conversations, and no locked devices. We can access each other's phones and emails—if we need to—without worrying about one person seeing something they shouldn't. There is a deep sense of security that comes with knowing that nothing is being hidden.

We know where each other is at any given time, who we're meeting, what we earn, and the assets we hold. We are completely honest and vulnerable in expressing our feelings, hurts, hopes, dreams and disappointments, no matter how uncomfortable it may feel sometimes. This level of openness has given us a sense of freedom and safety in our marriage and created an atmosphere where neither of us feels the need to second-guess or suspect the other. Instead of secrecy, there is trust. Instead of insecurity, there is confidence, and instead of emotional distance, there is deep connection. We don't just exist together—we are truly united.

The Power of Love in Fostering Vulnerability

At the heart of honesty and transparency is love. When you know you are deeply loved and fully accepted, it becomes easier to be vulnerable. Fear of judgment fades when you are confident that your spouse is for you, not against you.

As a woman, one of the things that has allowed me to be fully transparent and vulnerable with Julius is the deep security I feel in his love. From the moment we met and consistently through the years, he has demonstrated his unwavering love for me.

This assurance has freed me to be completely open with him without fear. *"There is no fear in love, but perfect love casts out all fear."* [22]

For me, as the man of the house, what has helped me maintain complete honesty and vulnerability is how Mary has consistently valued and appreciated my transparency. From the beginning, she never treated my openness as a sign of weakness but as a strength. This trust has created a safe environment where I can be fully myself without fear of judgment or being taken for granted.

If you want to create a space where honesty, transparency and vulnerability can thrive, commit to expressing and demonstrating your love for each other regularly. One of the greatest gifts you can give your spouse is the assurance that they are loved, no matter what. It's not enough to love your spouse—they need to *feel* loved. Learn their love language and speak it consistently. As both of you become more secure in each other's love—and in God's love for you—fear will begin to lose its hold, paving the way for deeper intimacy and lasting trust.

A thriving marriage is not one where two people guard themselves against each other but one where they surrender completely to the beauty of oneness. It is a relationship where

---

[22] 1 John 4:18

no part of you is off limits, where trust is never in question, and where both spouses know they are seen, heard, and fully loved. By choosing transparency, you create a marriage that is not only strong but also unshakable—one where both partners can flourish without fear, knowing they are in a relationship built on truth, love, and unwavering commitment. A marriage where both partners feel safe to be completely open and honest is a marriage where true intimacy flourishes.

No Secrets – No Barriers—Application Steps

☑ **Acknowledge and Share Your Fear**—Reflect on which of the fears mentioned in this chapter is currently hindering your ability to be completely honest, transparent, and vulnerable with your spouse. Openly share both your desire to build deeper intimacy and the specific fear that's holding you back. Ask for your spouse's support in overcoming this fear. Taking this step is an act of vulnerability in itself and a powerful way to begin breaking down emotional barriers.

☑ **Foster a Safe and Supportive Environment**—Talk with your spouse about how to create a space where both of you feel safe enough to be open and vulnerable. Agree to listen to each other without judgment and to take any concern raised by either of you seriously, no matter how insignificant it may seem. Commit to adopting the mindset that "if it matters to you, it matters to me." This approach helps your spouse feel valued, heard, and secure, making it easier to nurture honesty and transparency in your relationship.

☑ **Be Intentional About Fostering Transparency—** Schedule regular check-ins where you both set aside time to talk openly about your feelings, needs, hurts, and concerns. Remind each other that you are in this marriage for the long haul. Verbalize your love, loyalty, and commitment and use these moments to practice active listening, ask clarifying questions, and avoid making assumptions or judgements.

☑ **Pray Together Regularly—**Invite God into your journey toward greater honesty, transparency and vulnerability. Pray for wisdom, strength, and the courage to overcome fears that may hinder openness. As you both seek God's help, He will strengthen your bond and give you the grace to grow together.

15

BE CAREFUL WHO YOU HANG OUT WITH

Protecting Your Union Against Negative Outside Influence

Do not be misled. Bad company corrupts good character[23] and he who walks with the wise becomes wise, but the companion of fools suffers harm.[24] These timeless biblical truths carry profound weight, especially in marriage. Who we surround ourselves with shapes how we think, how we speak, and how we see—ourselves, our spouse, our relationship and the world. From the very start of our marriage, we made a deliberate choice to protect our sacred bond. We understood early on that while love and commitment are foundational, they are not self-sustaining. They require intentional protection—especially from negative external influences that can subtly, or sometimes abruptly, tear at the fabric of your union.

---

[23] 1 Corinthians 15:33
[24] Proverbs 13:20-21

One of the greatest threats to a marriage is not always conflict from within, but the unchecked influence of voices from without. Who you allow into your inner circle matters. The attitudes, opinions, and values of those closest to you can significantly shape how you view your spouse, your marriage, and even yourself.

The Power of Suggestion Is Real

The danger is not always in what is said explicitly, but in what is subtly implied. All it takes is one sentence spoken carelessly in passing to plant a seed of doubt or discontent in your heart. It could be something as casual as a work colleague saying, "You know Sarah's got a bit of a crush on you," and suddenly, someone you've never noticed before becomes oddly interesting. Or maybe you spend time with friends who constantly complain about their spouses, and before long, you start viewing your own partner through a more critical lens. It could be hanging out with women who believe all men are untrustworthy or with men who constantly reinforce the idea that women must be controlled or *"shown who's the boss."* Before long, you start to accommodate, excuse, and even embrace that way of thinking—often without realising it. Thoughts become beliefs, beliefs shape behaviour, and before long, that casual seed if not uprooted, becomes a weed threatening the garden of your relationship.

The Hidden Dangers of Third-Party Interference

Third-party interference is rarely obvious at first. It may come cloaked in concern or disguised as support. But its consequences can be devastating. Here are some ways they can cause damage:

The Seed of Doubt: It often starts innocently—a friend's opinion, a parent's comparison, or a co-worker's joke. But those words linger. You start questioning your spouse's intentions, over-analysing their words, or assuming the worst instead of the best. A once-loving perspective can become distorted by someone else's unresolved bitterness or personal bias.

Shifting Loyalties: Confiding more in others than your spouse can slowly shift your emotional allegiance. What should be sacred between you two becomes public property, and emotional distance begins to grow. This is often the first step toward emotional affairs—deep connections formed outside the covenant of marriage.

The Illusion of Objectivity: Those closest to us, especially family and friends, often lack true objectivity. They may only hear your side of the story, and out of love for you, may unintentionally fuel resentment toward your spouse. Their advice, though well-meaning, is not always wise or contextually grounded in the full truth of your situation.

Erosion of Intimacy and Trust: When you speak negatively about your spouse—especially in their absence—you chip away at the emotional safety in your marriage. It's like taking a hammer to the very foundation of trust you've worked so hard to build. You may feel justified in the moment, but the long-term consequences are rarely worth it.

Guarding the Sanctuary

Your marriage is not common ground—it's holy ground, a sanctuary. Treat it as sacred, because when you do, you protect it fiercely and intentionally. We are intentional about the words we speak—about, and to each other. Even in times of disagreement, we never make one another the punchline of a story.

We don't speak negatively about each other or argue in front of others—not before friends, family members, or even our children. Doing so only diminishes respect in their eyes, and it really does not matter who is right or wrong, we both lose out. In moments of frustration, it's tempting to vent to a friend, a family member, or even on social media. But what you share in anger might be twisted, misunderstood, or gossiped about. Well-meaning friends may offer advice that aligns more with their pain or personal bias than with wisdom or truth. And just like that, your private struggles become public issues.

We've also learned to filter the influence of family traditions and societal norms. While some inherited values are beautiful, others can become points of tension when they no longer serve the relationship. Early in our marriage, we made a bold decision: the only culture that would govern our home would be "God's Kingdom Culture"—rooted in biblical truth. It has made our home not just unique, but divinely grounded.

Build a Wall of Protection

The Bible teaches us that true love always protects.[25] This has been our guiding light from day one. Protecting our love has meant guarding what we say, who we share with, and whose opinions we allow into the intimate space of "us." We've never seen ourselves as "him and her," but as one unit. When one of us stumbles, both of us feel it. Our victories and setbacks are shared. That's why we've made it a non-negotiable to protect each other's image, reputation, and dignity always.

Build a wall of protection around your sacred space, not a mere fence. Not to isolate yourselves, but to protect the covenant you've made. Don't give everyone access to the private parts of your journey. Not everyone deserves a seat at the table of your marriage. Ultimately, protecting your union from negative outside influence is about honouring your commitment, and choosing unity above all else. A healthy marriage requires intentional shielding—because the world will not hesitate to pull at what you're not protecting.

---

[25] 1 Corinthians 13:7

Seek Help Wisely

Of course, there are times when counsel is necessary and there is absolutely no shame in getting help. In fact, there's wisdom in it. The Bible reminds us that where there is no counsel, people fall, but in the multitude of counsellors, there is safety. [26] We believe in the wisdom of godly, professional, or pastoral guidance. However, be careful who you turn to. Not every conversation is helpful and not every listener is trustworthy. Seek support from those who respect your relationship—those who are objective, discreet, and rooted in truth. A trained counsellor, a trusted mentor, or your pastor can offer invaluable guidance when needed. The key is to seek help with the goal of strengthening your marriage—not tearing down your partner.

Confidentiality in your relationship builds trust. When your spouse knows you won't broadcast their flaws or struggles, even in their worst moments, it fosters a sense of emotional security. It strengthens the foundation of your marriage. Protecting the sacred space of "us" is ultimately about honour. It's about cultivating a marriage marked by safety, respect, and unity. A marriage where love truly protects.

---

[26] Proverbs 11:14

Take Stock

Who are the people currently influencing your view of your spouse and your marriage? Are they helping you grow or sowing seeds of division? Do you hang out frequently with friends who never seem to have anything positive to say about their partners? How do you portray your spouse to third parties. What impression do you leave people with about your spouse. Remember, it's not just about what is said, but also what is unsaid. Are there conversations you've had about your spouse that, if they overheard, would hurt or dishonour them? Decide today to only speak, and act in ways that protect and strengthen your union not expose or tear it down.

Be careful Who You Hang Out With—Application Steps

☑ **Inner Circle Audit**—Make a list of the people who have direct influence in your life, or who you confide in about your relationship. Assess whether their influence supports or challenges your union. If it challenges it, you may want to stop sharing intimately with them.

☑ **Speak Honor Challenge**—For one week, speak only positive words about your spouse, both to them and about them. Reflect on the impact.

☑ **Cultivate Supportive Friendships**—Actively seek out and nurture friendships with other couples who share your values and respect the sanctity of marriage. These connections can provide mutual encouragement and accountability.

16

KEEP THE COMMUNICATION LINES OPEN

Maintaining Consistent, Candid and Caring Conversations

At the heart of every strong relationship is healthy communication. It is often called the lifeline of a marriage, and for good reason. Indeed, it really is the lifeline of every relationship. While conflicts in relationships may be caused by differences in opinions, they are kept alive and well by the party's inability to communicate effectively. We've seen this happen in so many relationships—what started as a minor misunderstanding spirals into a major issue, simply because one or both partners didn't feel heard and understood. When communication breaks down, everything breaks down.

The truth is, no marriage thrives on silence. When you don't talk openly about your feelings, needs, and concerns, assumptions start to take over. You assume your spouse knows what's bothering you. They assume you're fine because you haven't said otherwise. Before you know it, there's a growing emotional gap between you—one that becomes harder to bridge over time. That's why keeping the lines of communication open is not just a good idea; it's essential for a healthy, thriving marriage.

At its core, effective communication is about more than just talking. It's about expressing your thoughts and emotions honestly while also being fully present to listen and understand your spouse. It involves both speaking candidly with clarity and care and listening with empathy. It's not enough to simply exchange words—you need to connect through those words. This kind of connection only happens when both parties not only listen to respond but listen to understand and both feel safe enough to share their innermost thoughts without fear of judgment or dismissal.

When communication is effective, there's no guessing game. You don't have to wonder what your spouse is thinking or assume the worst because they've been silent. Instead, you create an atmosphere where both of you feel heard, valued, and understood. This doesn't mean you'll always agree, but it does mean that you'll approach disagreements with respect and a desire to find common ground.

Communication has not always been easy in our relationship. There have been times when we have both felt we were hitting our heads against a brick walk. We were speaking all right but were not communicating because we were more concerned about getting our points across, than listening to what the other person had to say in order to truly understand where they were coming from and to see their perspective. It's not always a question of one is right and the other is wrong. It's often just a question of different perspectives. When you can take a step back to truly listen to understand, then you are better positioned to reach the person where they are.

Mastering the Art of Effective Listening

One of the biggest misconceptions about communication is that it's all about talking, but in reality, listening is just as—if not more— important. And not just passive listening, but active listening. This means listening to understand, not just to respond. It's about giving your full attention to your spouse, setting aside distractions, and truly hearing what they are saying, even beyond the words they are speaking.

Too often, we listen with one ear while mentally preparing our response. We're ready to jump in and offer advice or defend our position before our spouse has even finished speaking. But when we do this, we miss the opportunity to fully understand where they're coming from. Active listening, on the other hand, slows us down. It invites us to put aside our own agenda and focus entirely not just on our spouse's words, but also their tone, body language and emotions. When we consider the research by Albert Mehrabian, which found that when it comes to face-to-face conversation, communication is 55% nonverbal—body language and facial expression, 38% vocal—tone and inflection, and only 7% verbal—the actual words spoken. What this means, is that if we are not fully present, we can miss about 93% of what is being communicated—that's huge!

A helpful principle to remember is Stephen Covey's "Seek first to understand, then to be understood" principle expounded on in his bestselling book *7 Habits of Highly Effective People*. This mindset shifts the focus from "How can I make my point?" to "How can I understand this person better?" When you approach conversations with your spouse with this posture, you create an environment where your spouse feels heard, valued, and respected. And the beautiful thing is—when someone feels truly understood, they're much more likely to reciprocate and listen in the same way.

What Helped Our Communication

Intentionally Developing our Communication Skills: In the words of George Bernard Shaw "The single biggest problem in communication is the illusion that it has taken place." We couldn't agree more. Because we are talking all day long and have been doing it almost all our lives, it's easy to think we naturally get good at communicating, after all we've had loads of practice, but this is not the case. Effective communication, the kinds that builds connections is a skill, and like every skill is learned.

The fact that you are a natural "people person", love people and love chatting with people does not automatically mean you are an effective communicator. Conversely the fact that you are perhaps an introvert and would rather be by yourself than engage with others does not necessarily mean you cannot be an effective communicator. You can start from where you are right now to start improving your communication skills. Read books, listen to podcasts, buy a course, find resources that focus on helping you cultivating your communication skills. Devour them and put your learnings into practice. Learning to communicate effectively is a lifelong process, but it is one of the most valuable skills you can develop for your marriage.

Inviting God into our Conversations: We'll be honest. There have been many times over the years when we've wondered, What's the point of talking? It felt like the more we tried to communicate, the further apart we drifted. Words were being misunderstood, and it was as if we were speaking completely different languages. The harder we tried to explain our perspective, the more the other person seemed to miss where we were coming from.

In those moments—after spending hours going in circles, feeling more frustrated and hurt—we learned to just stop. Stop trying to explain, to justify, to *convince*…and instead, invite God into the situation. We ask Him to take control, to soften our hearts, and to help us understand what the other person is really trying to say. When you invite God into your communication, He brings a level of grace, wisdom, and patience that goes beyond human effort. Praying together before discussing difficult topics allows God to guide your words and align your hearts, making space for understanding and healing even in the most challenging conversations.

Consistently Keeping the Communication Lines Open: As previously mentioned, there have been many times over the years when, despite our best efforts to resolve an issue— spending hours talking and trying to understand each other— it felt like we were only making things worse. In those moments, it was tempting to throw up our hands and ask, What's the point? But we never did. No matter how difficult it felt at times, we've chosen to keep the communication lines open because we know that is necessary if we want to enjoy and not just endure our marriage.

There were times when we had to step back from the issue and give it some space—praying about the situation and allowing God to work on our hearts. Sometimes, we found that certain things seemed to resolve themselves over time, but there were also times when we had to revisit the same issue again and again until we finally reached a place of understanding. If something remains an issue for one of us, we keep at it— continuing to communicate and work toward a solution.

So, no matter how discouraged you may feel right now about your communication with your spouse, don't give in to the temptation to shut down. There may be seasons when it feels like you're walking on eggshells or when the effort seems exhausting, but remember— when communication breaks down, everything else begins to break down too. Keep pressing on, because every step you take toward open and honest communication brings you one step closer to a stronger, more connected marriage.

Keep the communication Lines Open—Application Steps

☑ **Practice Active Listening**—Next time your spouse is speaking, pause the urge to interrupt, solve, or mentally prepare your reply. Instead, give your full attention— listening to both their words and their tone or body language. Reflect what you hear with phrases like, "What I'm hearing is…" or "It sounds like you're feeling…" to show understanding and validate their emotions.

☑ **Invite God into Your Conversations**—Whether before a difficult conversation or after a disagreement, prayer can align your hearts and guide your words. Make it a habit to pray before discussing sensitive topics and ask for wisdom to communicate with love and empathy.

☑ **Create a Safe Space for Difficult Conversations**—Set an atmosphere where both of you feel safe to express your honest thoughts and feelings without fear of judgment or criticism, even when the conversation gets uncomfortable.

Establish ground rules like "no interrupting," "no blaming," and "speak with kindness" to foster a judgment-free zone during important conversations.

17

HANDLE CONFLICT CONSTRUCTIVELY

Building Bridges, Not Walls

It's no exaggeration to say that misunderstandings and disagreements are inevitable in any close relationship. The key to a lasting, fulfilling marriage isn't the absence of conflict—it's knowing *how* to handle it when it comes. Conflict of itself is not a bad thing, it's how it is handled that could make it bad. Some people will avoid conflict at all costs, but avoiding conflict altogether often just pushes issues below the surface, allowing them to fester. Having the courage and caring enough for the relationship to deal with conflict when it arises is the pathway to a truly peaceful and happy relationship. So don't ignore them. A wiser approach is to learn the skills necessary to navigate conflict constructively so that, rather than tearing us apart, it brings us closer together.

Over the years, we've encountered our fair share of disagreements— some loud, some painful, and some that left us wondering if we'd ever find our way back to peace. There were moments that felt like breaking points, where "Is this it?" crossed our minds. But somehow, by God's grace and a stubborn commitment to see things through, we came out stronger. Not without bruises, but with deeper understanding, resilience, and a tighter bond. This isn't to suggest we've "arrived." Far from it. We're still growing, still learning. But one thing is certain: our marriage today is stronger because we chose to fight for each other, not with each other.

Shifting from Winning to Understanding

At the root of most conflict lies a simple truth: it's not about right or wrong—it's about perspective. Often, conflict surfaces when different needs, values, or expectations collide. One of the most transformative shifts we've made in our marriage is moving from a mindset of "winning the argument" to "understanding my partner." You can win a point and still lose your partner's heart. We've learned to value the connection over the correction, choosing empathy over ego and curiosity over criticism. And that starts with listening—not just hearing the words but truly *listening* to the heart behind them. Paying attention to body language, tone, and the emotion beneath the surface is just as important as the words being spoken.

Navigating the Heat of the Moment

When emotions are high, our natural instinct is to defend, deflect, or shut down. But reacting in anger often inflames the situation. One of the most loving things you can do in the moment is to pause. Sometimes, one of us will say, "Let's just leave this for now." That pause isn't avoidance—it's wisdom. It gives us time to calm down, gather our thoughts, and return to the conversation with more grace and clarity. Sometimes we've had to revisit over days before we found a resolve, but we've often found that when we revisit the issue later, things often look very different.

It's Not My Corner vs. Your Corner—It's Our Corner

We try to remind ourselves in tough conversations that this isn't me versus you. It's *us versus the issue*. There are no sides in our marriage—there's only one team. The moment we begin to see each other as adversaries, we've already started to lose. But when we remember that we're fighting for the same goal—mutual understanding and unity—we approach disagreements with a new lens. We stop focussing on who is wrong and start focussing on what we want. We find this shifts the focus from laying blame to finding resolution.

The Art of Compromise

Marriage is about give and take. Compromise isn't weakness—it's wisdom. It's the willingness to let go of our need to be right or have things our way in favour of what's best for *us*. Even when you feel absolutely convinced you are right, or that your way is the best way, seeking harmony might mean letting the other party have their way. Compromise says, "I value you more than I value the need to be right."

The Power of Forgiveness

Forgiveness is not optional if you want your relationship to thrive. And yes, it's hard—especially when the hurt runs deep. But we've discovered that holding on to offense only prolongs pain. Forgiveness doesn't mean what happened didn't matter—it means you choose healing over resentment. It's how we move forward. It's how we begin again. We've had to forgive each other many times. And we will have to do it again. But each time, it brings us back to each other. It restores peace, trust, and intimacy.

Practical Steps: Navigating Conflict with Care

We would like to share some intentional steps we've found helpful in managing conflict well

Listen with Empathy, Not Ego: Give your spouse your full attention—listen to understand, not to reply. Reflect back what you've heard to make sure you truly understand. "What I'm hearing is…" or "It sounds like you're feeling…" are helpful phrases.

Use Time-Outs Wisely: When things get heated, it's okay to pause. Step away, breathe, pray, reflect—and come back with a clearer mind and a softer heart.

Seek Common Ground, not a Win or Lose Approach: Approach conflict as partners, not opponents. Ask, "What outcome serves us both?" At the onset of the conversation, verbally remind yourselves that you are on the same side, and that what you are seeking is resolution. This immediately breaks down the defensive walls.

Pick the right moment: Raising a contentious matter immediately your spouse steps in from work might not be the best time. They may have had a hard day at work and not be in the best frame of mind to have that conversation. Read their mood. You don't have to always discuss an issue the moment it arises. You may have to just ignore it for the moment and raise it at a more opportune time.

Set the Scene with Care: Before diving into a difficult conversation, it can help to gently prepare your spouse by acknowledging that the topic may be uncomfortable. A simple, thoughtful approach like, *"There's something I'd like us to talk about. It might feel a bit uncomfortable, and honestly, I feel a little uneasy bringing it up—but I believe it's important for us to address so we can move forward together. Can we just be open and honest with each other for a moment?"* This kind of gentle framing lowers defences, sets a tone of mutual respect, and helps create a safe space for an honest and productive dialogue.

Reaffirm Your Commitment: After resolving a conflict, take a moment to reaffirm your love. A hug, a kiss, or a gentle touch can rebuild emotional closeness quickly.

Conflict isn't the enemy. Avoidance, resentment, and pride are. When handled with love, humility, and grace, conflict becomes a catalyst for growth. Every disagreement is an opportunity—to understand, to connect, and to love more deeply. So, build bridges, not walls. Choose unity over ego. And never forget you're on the same team.

Handling Conflict Constructively—Application Steps

☑ **Conflict Debrief Exercise**—After your next disagreement, take time to reflect together. Ask: What triggered this? What could we have done differently? What did we learn about each other?

☑ **Share your Communication Preferences**—Each of you should make a list of three ways you absolutely do not like to be communicated with. It could be 'don't raise your voice' or 'don't interrupt when I'm speaking' and exchange them, then both do your hardest to abide by them. If you need help with this, you may wish to obtain a Maxwell

DISC Personal Profile Report[27] which will spell out your communication "Dos" and "Do Nots" taking out the guesswork and helping you communicate with your spouse in their preferred manner.

☑ **Choose to Deflect Rather than Reflect**—Next time your spouse says something that feels offensive or hits you the wrong way, instead of mirroring their tone or energy right back—which often escalates the tension and leads to an emotional spiral— make a conscious choice to *deflect* rather than *reflect*. Pause, take a breath, and gently steer the conversation in a calmer, more constructive direction.

---

[27] www.candoacademy.net/ discover-your-true-self

18

KEEP THE SPARK ALIVE

Nurturing Romance and Intimacy

Think back to when you and your spouse first started dating, or even the early years in your marriage. Romance no doubt was effortless. Certainly, for us, time always stood still when we were with each other. There were days we spoke on the phone until we fell asleep, still holding the phone in our hand. We never seemed to tire of spending time with each other, holding hands, talking, it all came naturally. Our love was apparent to everyone around us.

After we got married, we decided to wait for at least a year before having out first child because we wanted to focus entirely on each other for at least a year before we had to deal with the distractions of children. We did not last a year though, but that's a different story ☺ The point is, in the early days, the excitement of discovering each other, going on dates, and spending time together makes it easy to keep the spark alive. But as the years go by, life inevitably gets busier. Careers demand more attention, children come into the picture, and responsibilities grow. The time and energy once devoted to romance can slowly fade into the background, replaced by routines, to-do lists, and exhaustion. Without even realizing it, the connection that once felt so natural can start to weaken.

This shift doesn't mean the love is gone or that the marriage is in trouble. It's simply the reality of life's evolving seasons. One of the biggest myths about love and romance is that if two people truly love each other, the spark will remain without any effort. That couldn't be further from the truth. Love is a choice we make every day, and nurturing intimacy requires intentionality. Just as a fire dies down if it's not tended to, romance will naturally wane if we don't take deliberate steps to keep it alive.

Why Keeping the Spark Matters

When romance and intimacy fade, couples can begin to feel more like roommates than lovers. The relationship may still function—bills get paid, the household runs, the children are taken care of—but emotional and physical closeness start to diminish. Over time, this can lead to frustration, loneliness, and even resentment. Sadly, one of the most significant risks of neglecting intimacy is that it opens the door for infidelity. Many affairs don't happen because someone sets out to be unfaithful, but rather because they begin to crave the attention, affection, and excitement they once felt in their marriage. While this is never an excuse for betrayal, it highlights the importance of prioritizing connection and keeping the relationship fulfilling for both parties.

Being Intentional About Romance

A thriving marriage requires more than just love—it requires effort, creativity, and a willingness to keep pursuing each other, no matter how many years have passed. Because romance won't maintain itself, couples must be deliberate in keeping it alive. This does not necessarily mean grand gestures all the time, but rather, small consistent actions that show love, appreciation, and desire for one another. However, it's important to remember that what excites or fulfils you may not be the same for your spouse. Don't assume their needs mirror yours.

For one partner, a simple glance at their spouse stepping out of the shower might be enough to ignite passion, while for the other, romance is built through thoughtful gestures throughout the day. A loving text message, an unexpected call just to say "I love you," a shoulder massage while they do the dishes, or lingering a little longer in a welcome-home hug—these small moments create intimacy and connection. The key is to communicate openly about what makes each of you feel loved and desired, and to respect that both partners' needs are equally valid.

It's not uncommon to hear complaints like, "My spouse doesn't satisfy me sexually" or "We don't make love often enough." However, viewing intimacy as something your spouse does for you rather than something you experience together can be problematic. For some, physical intimacy is the main focus, while for others, the emotional connection matters just as much—if not more. If your spouse frequently expresses frustration about you not spending enough quality time together, or feeling emotionally disconnected, and you pay no attention, only engaging with them intimately when you want sex, and then complain that you are not getting enough sex because they don't seem to be co-operative in those moments, that's not fair or balanced. It means you're prioritizing your own needs while neglecting theirs.

True intimacy isn't about just getting your own needs met—it's about mutual fulfilment. What excites you or fills your bucket might be completely different from what excites or satisfies your partner. That's why it's so important to take the time to truly understand each other's needs and desires.

Have open, honest conversations. Share what turns you on with your spouse and let them know how they can meet your sexual and emotional needs. Don't assume or just expect them to know—most people don't read minds. Just as importantly, make the effort to understand your spouse's needs and prioritize them too. When both partners feel seen and heard, intimacy deepens—naturally and meaningfully.

Some Ways to Intentionally Nurture Romance:

Date Nights – Set aside regular time just for the two of you. Whether it's going out for dinner, taking a walk, or having a cozy night in with a movie, what matters is prioritizing your time together.

Surprise Each Other – Thoughtful surprises keep the relationship exciting. A sweet note, a small gift, or planning an unexpected outing can go a long way in making your spouse feel special.

Physical Touch Matters – Hugs, kisses, holding hands, and simple acts of affection help maintain emotional closeness. Don't reserve intimacy only for the bedroom—make touch a regular part of your daily life.

Flirt and Have Fun – Keep playfulness alive in your marriage. Send a flirty text, share an inside joke, or reminisce about the early days of your relationship. Get some sexy lingerie and put on a sexy dance show for your spouse.

Look Good for Each Other – While inner beauty and character matter most, physical attraction still plays a big role in marriage. We shouldn't stop caring about our appearance once we've said, "I do." It's important to continue putting in effort—not just for ourselves, but also for our spouse.

Communicate Your Needs – Romance isn't a one-size-fits-all affair. What makes one person feel loved may not work for the other. Talk openly about what makes you feel desired and connected and be willing to meet your spouse's needs.

The Myth of Spontaneous Romance

Many people resist the idea of planning for romance, believing it should always happen naturally. But the truth is, most important aspects of life—our careers, parenting, even spiritual growth—require effort and intentionality. Why should marriage be any different? Scheduling date nights or making a conscious effort to be romantic doesn't make it any less special; rather, it ensures that amidst life's busyness, your relationship remains a priority.

It's also important to note that while it doesn't matter who takes the initiative to plan date nights or create quality time, if the effort always comes from one party, the other may eventually feel like romance isn't important to them. Over time, this can create emotional distance, as no one wants to feel like they are forcing their spouse to engage in something they have no interest in. Even if romantic gestures aren't naturally your thing, or you're content to go without intimacy until you desire sex, consider how that might make your spouse feel. If the only time you express interest in them is when you want something, they may start to feel used rather than cherished. However, when both parties are intentional about nurturing intimacy—whatever that looks like for your relationship— both will feel valued, desired, and emotionally fulfilled.

The Reward of Intentional Love

When both partners commit to keeping the spark alive, the marriage remains strong, fulfilling, and full of joy. Rather than growing apart, you continue to grow together. No matter how long you've been married, it's never too late to rekindle the romance. Start today—be intentional, put in the effort, and watch your relationship flourish like never before.

Keep The Spark Alive – Application Steps

☑ **Schedule Regular Date Nights—** This could be weekly, monthly, or as often as life allows—make it a priority and take turns planning it. One month you choose, the next it's your spouse's turn. It can be as simple as a picnic in the park, a new restaurant, a surprise getaway, or just takeout and a candlelit movie night in. The key is intentionality — no rescheduling, no distractions, just quality time together.

☑ **Create a Daily 10-Minute Connection Ritual—**Set aside at least 10 minutes every day to connect meaningfully. This could be morning coffee together before work, a cuddle or chat before bed (without screens!) or a daily "How was your day?" check-in. Consistency in small things builds deep intimacy over time.

☑ **Leave Room For Each Other—**Over committing yourselves and cramming your calendars and days with activities, no matter how productive could be damaging to your love life. Not only could it lead to stress—which is a romance killer—it leaves no room for spontaneity and little room to really prioritise each other. Leave room in your calendar for your spouse's interruptions.

☑ **Break the routine with unexpected acts of love**—Leave a love note in their bag or car, send a flirty text during the day, plan an at-home spa night, have flowers delivered to them at work or at home (if they are at home) while you are at work.

19

CHOOSE JOY AND INVEST IN HAPPINESS

Not Just Enduring but Enjoying Your Marriage

A marriage without joy is like a car running without oil—it might keep going for a while, but eventually, the engine will wear out. In the same way, it's not enough to simply remain in a relationship; if you want to truly divorce-proof your marriage, you must be committed to staying happy together.

Staying Is Not the Same as Thriving

The goal is not simply staying together but thriving together. Deciding to stay and see your marriage through is honourable—and absolutely encouraged. But staying together without joy is no real victory. Being married for 30, 40, or 50 years is worth celebrating only if, after all those years, you still enjoy each other's company, still laugh together, and still look forward to seeing each other at the end of a long day.

It's easy to slip into the role of a martyr in marriage, especially when children, financial stress, or personal disappointments pile up. One or both spouses may sacrifice their happiness in the name of duty, convincing themselves it's noble to "just endure" for the sake of the family. And while short-term sacrifices are sometimes necessary, long-term unhappiness quietly chips away at the foundation of a relationship.

People don't always walk away from marriages because everything is in chaos. Often, they walk away because they lose hope that joy can ever return. That's why choosing and investing in happiness isn't a luxury—it's a necessity.

Don't Wait for Happiness—Create It

Happiness isn't something you stumble into; it's something you build, brick by brick. Waiting for the "perfect" season when life slows down or gets easier only delays joy. Instead, carve out space for it—even in the middle of chaos. Like anything valuable, happiness requires intentional effort. It doesn't just happen. It's cultivated, nurtured, and fiercely protected.

Think of happiness as a joint bank account—you both need to make deposits if you expect to make withdrawals. Without intentional investment, the emotional reserves of your relationship can quickly run dry, leaving space for resentment, fatigue, and disconnection to take root.

In our relationship, Julius is the one who brings the humour. He's always ready to laugh at himself—and usually harder than anyone else. Sometimes it's spontaneous; other times, you can tell he's being deliberate about creating joy in our home. We all love that about him! It's actually one of the things that first attracted me to him. I tease him often about how "dry" his jokes are, especially because he laughs so hard telling them. But even when the joke falls flat, his joy is contagious. Our kids, now grown, still fondly recall those silly stories and the sound of his laughter. Often, we're not even laughing at the joke anymore—we're laughing at how much he's laughing in telling the joke. It's wonderful—Laughter is good medicine for the soul. [28]

You however don't need to be naturally funny or be a comedian to bring joy into your home. Even with busy schedules, parenting demands, and long to-do lists, you can choose to laugh together more often. Watch a comedy every Friday night, take a walk together, revisit something you both love. Find your happy place— and go there often.

Don't Outsource Your Happiness

No spouse can meet every need. If you expect them to, disappointment is inevitable. We often hear people say, *"They just don't make me happy anymore."* But here's the truth: placing

---

[28] Proverbs 17:22

your happiness entirely in someone else's hands is giving away something too valuable. Happiness is one of the most sought-after human experiences—so why entrust it to someone else?

You must take ownership of your own happiness. Of course, communicate openly with your spouse about what fills and drains your emotional tank. Support each other in creating joy. But remember, your happiness is your responsibility. Don't just commit to staying together—commit to being happy together. Looking for happiness outside your marriage often leads to disillusionment. The grass might seem greener elsewhere, but every lawn needs tending. If you stop watering your own, it will wither too. Care for your marriage like a garden—nurture it, weed out the negativity, and you'll enjoy its fruits.

We've walked through seasons where things felt bleak. There were moments we questioned whether we'd ever enjoy each other again, or if we'd spend the rest of our lives just co-existing, walking on eggshells. But we made a shared decision—not only to stay, but to stay happy because we both deserve to be happy, to enjoy each other again. Today, we can honestly say our love is sweeter and stronger than when we started. No, it's not as intense or passionate as it was in the beginning—we don't spend hours chatting about nothing anymore—who has time for that? 😊 But it's deeper, and richer, and for that we are genuinely thankful.

Reflect and Reconnect

If joy feels distant right now, take time to reflect together using these questions:

What brings us joy right now? Identify the moments—big or small— that bring happiness. Are you nurturing those moments? If not, how can you be more intentional?

What sacrifices are we making? Are either of you sacrificing your happiness in ways that feel heavy or unappreciated? How can you express this honestly and find a healthier balance?

How are we contributing to each other's happiness? Are you regularly making emotional "deposits"? What simple things can you do to lift your partner's spirits?

When did we last laugh together? Is laughter part of your rhythm? What fun, light-hearted moments can you plan or rediscover?

What's blocking our joy? Whether it's unresolved conflict, unrealistic expectations, or burnout—identify what's getting in the way and commit to tackling it together.

Choose Joy—Together

Choosing joy isn't about having the perfect circumstances. It's about setting the right priorities. Happy couples aren't those who never argue or struggle. They're the ones who keep showing up for each other—who choose love, pursue joy, and protect their peace.

So yes—choose to stay. But also choose to smile more, laugh often, forgive faster, and play together. Dream, dance, be silly. Prioritize joy. Because when happiness lives in your home, love has room to breathe.

Choose Joy and Invest in Happiness—Application Steps

☑ **Revisit Your Favourite Memories**—Take a night to reminisce about the early days of your relationship or your happiest moments together. Share the memories that still make you smile. Afterward, ask each other: "How can we create new memories like these today?"

☑ **Laugh Together Challenge**—Find one activity or event that will make you both laugh in the next week. Whether it's watching a comedy together, playing a silly game, getting some jokes off the internet and reading them to each other, it really does not matter what it is. Make time to laugh together and stick to it, no matter how awkward or *forced* it might appear initially.

☑ **Create a "Happiness Vision" for Your Marriage**—Sit down together and talk about what happiness in your marriage looks like. What makes you both feel fulfilled? What changes would you like to see in how you interact? Write these down and revisit them every few months to see how you're progressing.

20

CHOOSE CONTENTMENT OVER COMPARISON

Gratitude Fuels Love— Comparison Drains It

It's easy to fall into the trap of comparison—especially in a world where other people's lives are constantly on display. With just a few swipes, we can see Instagram images and reels of beautifully curated marriages, picture-perfect date nights, and couples who seem to have it all together. What we fail to appreciate is that what we're often seeing is a highlight—not the full story.

Social media, for all its benefits, often amplifies this danger. We're fed a steady diet of polished images and feel-good captions that can distort our sense of reality. It's important to remind yourself often: *what you're seeing is not the whole story.* No one posts the argument they had the night before or the silent treatment that lasted all weekend. You don't see the work that went into rebuilding trust after disappointment or the years of effort it took to get to that happy anniversary post. Real relationships take work—messy, beautiful, sacred work.

The truth is every relationship has its own rhythm, its own story, and its own unique beauty. And when you start comparing yours to someone else's, you blur your vision. You stop seeing the beauty in your own journey and instead begin measuring your life and your spouse against someone else's edited moments. Success is subjective, so define your own success, based on your own values and aim for that.

Don't compare your spouse to anyone else, including your parents. While it's natural to want to re-create aspects of a positive upbringing, remember: your wife is not your mum, and your husband is not your dad. Comments like "My mum always did…" or "My dad never…" can feel like criticism and may cause hurt or resentment. They not only make your spouse feel inadequate but can also create unnecessary tension between them and your parents.

Our relationship is not in competition with any other couple's. Our family is unique, and we've chosen to chart our own course, and beat our own path. Trying to "keep up with the Joneses" only creates unnecessary pressure, a sense of lack, and unfulfillment. We don't want that. We've chosen instead to build a life that's meaningful to *us*—a life that aligns with our shared values, not anyone else's standards.

The Bible tells us that godliness with contentment is great gain.[29] Like we said before, as Christians, we fully embrace the principles in the bible, and endeavour to live our lives by them. So, we 100% embrace the value of contentment. We must make the point that it's not about settling—it's about choosing to value what you do have, not constantly yearning for what you think you lack. It's not that you don't strive for more and better, but you learn to look at your partner through eyes of appreciation rather than constant expectation. When you make that shift, you begin to see how far you've both come, the battles you've fought and won, and the growth you've experienced as a couple.

One of the most powerful ways we've discovered to guard our hearts against comparison is practicing gratitude. Gratitude shifts your focus like nothing else can. In an instant, you can go from feeling extremely miserable, to feeling inexplicable joy, just by shifting from whatever energy you were in, to gratitude. Gratitude pulls your attention away from what's missing and directs it toward what's present. It invites joy into your everyday moments and when you practice gratitude together as a couple, it deepens your emotional connection.

Not long ago, I came home feeling completely drained. It had been one of those days where everything seemed to go wrong, and I was venting about how terrible it had been—yes, we did

---

[29] 1 Timothy 6:6-8

say we're not perfect! 😊 As I continued to grumble, Mary gently interrupted and said, "Tell me 10 things you're grateful for today." My immediate response was, "Honey, I'm really not in the mood for gratitude right now—I've had a rough day." But if you know Mary, you'll know that once she sets her mind on something, she doesn't back down. So, reluctantly, I started listing. To my surprise, by the time I reached the fifth item, my mood had already started to lift. The heaviness I'd brought home with me began to lose its grip. By the time I got to number ten, not only was I feeling lighter, but I also didn't want to stop counting.

Now it wasn't that Julius didn't know the power of gratitude, but sometimes, when you're caught in the middle of your own storm, you lose sight of what's still good. That's why we all need people in our lives who can lovingly remind us—coaches, mentors, or spouses—who see what we can't because we're too close to the situation. As the saying goes, "You can't see the picture when you're in the frame." It's one thing to know the value of gratitude; it's another to *recognise* the moments when it's most needed. The Bible reminds us to give thanks in all things,[30] so we've chosen to make gratitude a daily habit and we've seen firsthand how it shifts our hearts and renews our perspective.

---

[30] 1 Thessalonians 5:18

While comparison and discontent distract you from the blessings in your own garden by constantly making you peer over the fence at someone else's, gratitude reminds you to pause, to notice, and to celebrate even the small things. The benefit of this seemingly small, insignificant act is staggering. A 2018 White Paper titled *The Science of Gratitude* published by The Greater Good Science Centre outlines several benefits to practicing gratitude, including increased happiness and positive mood, more satisfaction with life, less materialism, less likelihood to experience burnout, better physical health, better sleep, less fatigue, greater resilience, better emotional well-being, better relationships, and the list goes on.

As mentioned in a previous chapter, the company we keep matters tremendously as it greatly influences who we become. Avoid those who speak negatively about their partners or constantly complain. Their words may begin to shape your expectations and create silent discontent in your own heart. You can train yourself to see the glass half full rather than half empty. You can practice gratitude intentionally until it becomes your default lens. And when you do, you'll begin to see the beauty in your ordinary days. You'll treasure your spouse more deeply, and you'll find greater satisfaction in the life you're building—together.

We often remind ourselves of the fictitious story of a man lamenting about his lack of shoes, until he saw a man with no feet. When you feel tempted to complain about your spouse and their habits that drive you up the wall, ask yourself, *"would I rather have no spouse?"* When the children are *"driving you crazy"* with their mess or constant squabbling, ask yourself *"would I rather be childless?"* Make it a habit to always look for something to be grateful for in every situation. You will be amazed at just how full your life really is.

Choose Contentment Over Comparison— Application Steps

☑ **Incorporate Gratitude into Every Day**—Find time every day to practice gratitude, either alone or together. It could be during mealtime, before you go to bed, or as you go for your daily walk. Get the kids involved. Everyone should take turns to say one thing they are grateful for each day.

☑ **Social Media Fast or Filter**—Take a short break from social media or intentionally unfollow accounts that trigger comparison. Replace that time with reading, prayer, or meaningful connection with your spouse.

☑ **Celebrate Small Wins Together**—Set aside time weekly or monthly to celebrate something—no matter how small. A tough week survived, a good conversation had, a goal met, or even just being consistent in showing up for each other. Let celebration be part of your rhythm.

21

CHALLENGE YOUR BELIEFS AND TRADITIONS

Letting Go of Stereotypes to Build Something New

We all carry a past. Each of us steps into marriage with a history shaped by family, culture, and personal experiences—some uplifting, others not so much. These influences shape how we think, what we value, and even how we expect relationships to function. But here's the truth: not every belief or tradition held is helpful. Some, if left unexamined and unchallenged, can become stumbling blocks. It takes courage and wisdom to reflect on these inherited ideas and ask, "Does this still serve us?"—or even more boldly, "Was it ever really right for us?"

We often think of the story of a woman who always cut the ends off her ham before cooking. When her husband asked why, she shrugged and said, "That's how my mum always did it." Intrigued, they asked her mother, who gave the same answer. Finally, they turned to the grandmother, who laughed and said, "I only did that because my pan was too small!" This light-hearted tale perfectly illustrates a deeper truth: just because something has been done a certain way for generations doesn't mean it's the best way—or the right way—for your relationship.

Early in our marriage, the differences in our cultural backgrounds were easy to overlook—we were in love, and love made everything feel seamless. But as time passed and life got more complex—especially when we began raising children—those differences started to show. While we agreed on many principles, the way we implemented them sometimes clashed, particularly around disciplining the children. It became a point of tension that took time, constant communication, and humility to work through.

We started to notice subtle contrasts whenever friends or family came over. Sometimes, a simple passing comment would highlight something different about the way we did things in our home. Not wrong—just unique. And that's the key: being *different* isn't a problem; it's often the very beginning of discovering what truly works for *you*.

We remember one particular evening when some close family friends joined us for dinner. After we ate, Julius got up to help clear the table and started washing the dishes. Our male friend raised an eyebrow and jokingly said, "You do dishes? I don't do dishes!" We all laughed, let it slide, and carried on with the evening. Fast forward a few months—this same couple hosted us at their place, and to our surprise, after dinner, our friend quietly rolled up his sleeves and began doing the dishes himself. We couldn't resist teasing him about his earlier comment. His response? With a sheepish grin he said, "Well, my brother, I do dishes now. I got tired of hearing 'I have a headache' every time I made a move."

Now, here's the thing: if Julius hadn't been secure in himself and confident in what works for our home, that offhand remark from our friend could have sparked doubt. It could have led to him questioning himself or even unnecessary arguments. He could have questioned why he was doing the dishes, when other men don't. Thank goodness, he didn't. We've learned not to let what others do dictate what we do. Sometimes, while you're busy comparing yourself to someone else and possibly envying them, they might actually be watching you for inspiration and envying you. So be careful not to let someone else's expectations, beliefs, traditions—or even their jokes—make you second-guess the harmony you've built in your own relationship. Stick with what works for *you*.

Questions like should the husband bear all the financial responsibility, even if the wife is also working? Is it the wife's "duty" to handle all household chores, even if she works full time just like her husband? Can cause a rift in the family if one is not careful. In some cultures, even the idea of a husband doing chores might be frowned upon—but we've found that in our home, partnership works far better than role-play. We made a conscious decision early on: rather than defaulting to "my culture" or "your culture," we would adopt a new one— *God's Kingdom culture*. That decision has stood us in good stead, helping us navigate differences by asking not what tradition says, but what truth says. Our shared faith became our compass, and we've built our home on biblical values that serve both of us well.

We still have designated responsibilities, but our attitude is simple: *if something needs doing, just get it done*. Whether it's dishes or finances, cooking or kids' homework, we work as a team. We're also intentional about raising our sons with the same mindset—servant-hearted, responsible, and never too proud to help. We want them to be the kind of men who make great husbands and leaders one day. 😊

Another area we had to grow in was understanding how we each gave and received love. What felt like love to one of us might be invisible to the other. We had to spell it out—write down what made each of us feel valued and talk through it. Once we did, it became clear: if it matters to one, it should matter to *both*.

Our home today is a blend of different cultures, shaped not by outside expectations but by intentional decisions. We've crafted a rhythm that fits us. We don't allow societal norms or even well-meaning advice from others dictate our dynamic. We take what serves us, leave what doesn't, and keep growing.

Letting go of limiting beliefs and traditions isn't a one-time decision—it's an ongoing journey. It calls for honest conversations, open hearts, and a willingness to grow together rather than cling to the familiar. In marriage, we're not just co-existing, we're co-creating. And the most beautiful marriages are built by two people who dare to honour the past while boldly shaping a future that reflects who they truly are—together.

So, hold your beliefs and traditions with an open hand. Let them be examined, challenged, and if necessary, released. Because it's in that space of humility and openness that something new, something beautiful, can begin.

Challenge Your Beliefs and Traditions—Application Steps

☑ **Identify and Evaluate Your Traditions**—Consider the triggers for most of the conflict or arguments in your home. Reflect on the beliefs and traditions you hold that could subtly be at play causing you to respond or react the way you do and challenge them. Ask yourself "why do I think this way?" and more importantly "is this way of thinking serving us?"

☑ Each of you list three beliefs or traditions you brought into the marriage related to key areas of married life, for example finances, raising the kids, roles in the home etc. Initiate conversation about the origin of your individual beliefs and traditions and each of you share your perspectives. This could be the first step to starting to shift those perspectives.

☑ **Seek Understanding Over "Being Right":** When differences arise from ingrained beliefs, prioritize understanding your spouse's perspective and the value it holds for them, rather than immediately defending your own as the "correct" way.

22

ESTABLISH BOUNDARIES TO PROTECT YOURSELVES

It's Not a Sign of Weakness, it's Wisdom

Several years ago, shortly after we got married, Julius was working as a minicab driver in the London area. One evening, he picked up an elderly passenger who, as it turned out, was our neighbour. The gentleman appeared slightly intoxicated, a bit unsteady on his feet, but managed to settle into the car. As often happens during cab rides, a conversation sparked, and marriage came up.

The man shared that he'd been married for over twenty years—what felt like a lifetime to us at the time. Curious, Julius asked if he had any regrets. He replied, "Yes... about twenty years ago, I cheated on my wife." It was a sobering confession, but assuming the years had brought healing, Julius gently commented, "She must have forgiven you." "Oh yes," the man replied, "she forgave me... but she reminds me every now and then." When they arrived at his destination, the man paid his fare, stepped out of the car, and began to walk away. He however then paused, turned back, leaned into the car with a heavy breath laced with alcohol, locked eyes with Julius, and with raw sincerity said "Believe me, son—it's not worth it. Never betray your wife like I did." Then he walked off.

Julius shared this encounter with me when he got home, as he does everything else, and although he never saw the gentleman again, he often recalls the experience— especially when we hear of a couple breaking up because of infidelity— Trust, once broken, is never quite the same.

Why Boundaries Matter

The word infidelity carries a heavy weight—broken promises, deep betrayal, shattered trust. It doesn't just hurt the couple; it tears through the fabric of their shared life, often leaving ruins in its path. We've never assumed, "It could never happen to us." That kind of thinking breeds complacency. We've learned that hearts can be more vulnerable than we realise—especially when we stop paying attention. Temptation rarely shows up with flashing lights. More often, it sneaks in through seemingly harmless interactions, small compromises, or innocent conversations that gradually cross lines we never intended to cross.

Our goal isn't to live in fear, constantly on edge. Rather, we choose *intentional vigilance*. We believe in building strong, clear boundaries—not because we're insecure, but because we're wise. And because we value what we've built too much to leave it unguarded.

Our Boundaries in Practice

One of the most powerful safeguards we've put in place is protecting our emotional intimacy. We've committed to saving our deepest conversations—our fears, dreams, and vulnerabilities—for each other. We are each other's strongest confidants and each other's prayer partners. When emotional intimacy is shared too freely outside the marriage, even in seemingly harmless friendships, it can quietly open the door to emotional attachment. The digital world has complicated this even further. Social media, messaging apps, and online interactions make it easier than ever to form connections outside of the marriage.

We've also made simple, practical choices that help us stay on course. We avoid being alone in private—completely secluded from everyone else—with someone of the opposite sex. This could be in a room with the door shut, or even in a car. While we might give or accept a ride from a member of the opposite sex under circumstances where we would be along in the car, we agree not to make it a habit. We want to limit that proximity, which breeds familiarity and could lead to something unintended particularly in seasons where you might be particularly vulnerable because of other things going on. We don't take personal calls from a member of the opposite sex after certain hours. It's all about safeguarding ourselves and our relationship.

Our social circle plays a key role too. We surround ourselves with people who respect marriage, who honour their vows, and who help us protect ours. These are friends who would challenge us if we were drifting, not cheer us on blindly. And most importantly, we've created a culture of *radical honesty* in our home. We talk about EVERYTHING. If one of us is feeling particularly vulnerable or think someone is making a pass at them or being flirtatious, we share it. Evil thrives in darkness and so we leave no room for secrets or shadows. In the clear light of truth, trust has space to grow, and infidelity can't thrive.

Boundaries aren't about fear. They're about freedom—the freedom to love each other well, to protect what you've built, and to live without regrets. We don't claim to be perfect, but we've shared with you what has worked and continues to work for us. Take what you believe will serve you, and leave the rest, but do whatever is required to protect your marriage. Remember trust, once broken, is incredibly hard to restore.

Establish Boundaries to Protect Yourselves — Application Steps

☑ **Define Your Boundaries Together**—Sit down with your spouse and openly discuss what emotional, physical, and digital boundaries are important to each of you and agree the boundaries you will both adhere to.

☑ **Perform a Relationship Audit**—Take a look at your current friendships, work dynamics, and digital habits. Are there any connections that make you or your spouse uncomfortable? Any blurred lines that need redefining? Talk about them and make any necessary changes.

☑ **Practice Radical Transparency**—Prioritise sharing your deepest feelings and vulnerabilities primarily with each other, being mindful of forming undue emotional connections outside your marriage.

23

TAKE RESPONSIBILITY FOR YOUR ACTIONS

Owning Your Part in The Story

When things aren't going well—or not as well as we would like—it's natural to look outside ourselves for both the cause and the solution. It's a very human tendency to make excuses for our own behaviour while placing the blame on others. Somehow, it's never really our fault; it's always someone else's—or at least, it's mostly their fault. We are often far more gracious with ourselves, judging ourselves by our intentions, while judging others by their actions. We like to imagine that we're the ones who have it all together, while everyone else is flawed. But here's a reality check: humans are inherently imperfect—and that includes you too!

Living closely with another human being means our flaws and weaknesses—those parts of us we might hide from the world—are laid bare. Marriage strips away the masks we sometimes wear, revealing our true selves. You can however take heart in knowing that imperfection is not something to be ashamed of. It's part of the shared human experience. Your spouse isn't perfect either, so you are in good company. As recorded in the Bible, Adam and Eve were both naked and not ashamed.[31] This is a beautiful picture of what marriage should be—a relationship where both partners can be completely open, honest and vulnerable, even in their imperfection.

When conflict arises, it's incredibly tempting to deflect blame. We reach for phrases like, "If you hadn't provoked me...," "See what you made me do...," or, "If you hadn't said it like that..." In the heat of the moment, blaming someone else feels easier than owning our part. Even when we do apologise, it's often laced with an excuse: "Sorry I hung up on you, but I found what you were saying really annoying," or, "I'm sorry I snapped, but I've had such a rough day." In our desire to protect ourselves, we end up building walls—walls of defensiveness and distance between us and the person we vowed to love and cherish. As Mary often says, never spoil an apology with an excuse.

In our minds, we justify it by thinking, *If they just understood why I reacted the way I did, maybe they'd change and avoid causing it next time.* But when we explain away our behaviour by blaming someone else's actions, we do two damaging things. First, we hand over our power, allowing their actions to control how we respond, how we feel, and what we say. Why would we

---

[31] Genesis 2:25

willingly give someone else that much control over us? Second, we give ourselves permission to repeat that behaviour. Essentially, we're saying, *"If you upset me again, I reserve the right to react badly."* Until we choose to take 100% responsibility for our own actions—regardless of what the other person says or does—we remain trapped in a cycle of destructive behaviour. As coaches, one of the first things we tell our clients is this: "If you genuinely want to create lasting change in your life, you must be willing to take 100% responsibility for your actions." They often protest, "But I can't control everything that happens to me!" And they're right—you can't. But you can always control how you respond. In the words of Allanah Hunt, *"It is only when you take responsibility for your life that you discover how powerful you truly are."*

When we refuse to take responsibility, several damaging things begin to happen in a relationship:

Trust starts to erode: If one or both partners constantly deflect blame, it becomes hard to feel emotionally safe.

Resentment builds: Small unresolved issues pile up, turning into bitterness over time.

Communication breaks down: Without ownership, real understanding and reconciliation cannot happen.

Emotional intimacy is lost: Vulnerability thrives in honesty, but it withers when pride and denial take over.

Cyclical arguments form. Without taking ownership, the same issues resurface again and again, often escalating more each time.

Over time, a marriage where blame thrives becomes a cold, lonely place.

Barriers to Taking Responsibility

Why is it so hard sometimes to own our part in things? Here are some common barriers:

Ego: Our ego wants to protect our image, even at the expense of intimacy. It whispers, *"Don't let them see you mess up."* Our ego makes us think we can't admit we are wrong because it makes us appear weak or inadequate. Some people have the wrong notion that their value is tied to always being right. This is of course not true. Real strength lies in humility; in being able to admit your own fault. That's not weakness, it's maturity and courage. Remember that true love isn't about protecting your ego—it's about protecting your connection.

Stubbornness: This can be one of the greatest barriers to taking responsibility. When we are stubborn, we dig our heels in, refusing to budge even when we know, deep down, that we are wrong. It becomes less about seeking truth or building connection, and more about "winning" or "saving face." The problem is, in marriage, when one person "wins," the relationship often loses. Stubbornness keeps conflicts alive much longer than necessary, turning small misunderstandings into deep wounds. It blocks forgiveness and growth, creating a silent, simmering tension that pushes spouses apart. Overcoming stubbornness requires humility—the willingness to lay down our pride for the sake of peace and intimacy. It's about choosing to do right over being right.

Fear of Rejection: This is another powerful barrier to taking ownership. Admitting our mistakes makes us feel vulnerable. There's a real fear that if our spouse sees our flaws too clearly, they might love us less, or worse, reject us entirely. As a result, some people hide behind defensiveness, blame, or withdrawal, thinking it's safer. But the truth is, vulnerability is the bridge to deeper intimacy. When we are brave enough to own our failures and fears, we invite our spouse to do the same, and we create a relationship built on authenticity, not pretence.

A desire to have our own way: When getting what we want becomes the priority, we naturally resist acknowledging when we are wrong, because doing so might mean giving up control, admitting defeat, or not having things turn out the way we envisioned. Marriage thrives on mutuality—on the ability to serve, to yield, and to compromise. Always insisting on having our way undermines the spirit of unity and leaves the other person feeling unseen, unheard, and unloved. Overcoming this tendency means shifting our mindset from "me" to "we," recognising that our highest goal is not personal victory, but shared success in our relationship.

Choosing a Better Way

It always takes two to tango. Before you rush to remove the speck from your spouse's eye, take a good look at the log in your own.[32] As tempting as it might be, resist the urge to downplay your own role in the conflict while amplifying your spouse's. Even if you believe they are 99.9% responsible for the tension between you, take full ownership of your 0.1%. That small step is powerful—it's often the key that opens the door to healing and reconciliation. You'll find that when you take responsibility, defences start to crumble, and your spouse's heart begins to soften toward you. Taking ownership doesn't diminish your value; it elevates it. It shows maturity, a willingness to grow, and a love that extends beyond self-protection to truly safeguarding the relationship.

In marriage, the goal should never be to win arguments but to win each other's hearts. Winning an argument but losing intimacy is a hollow victory. True success is creating a marriage where humility, honesty, and forgiveness flow freely between two imperfect people who are committed to loving each other well. Taking responsibility also means making genuine amends.

Saying "I'm sorry" matters, but what matters even more is following those words with changed behaviour. The old saying "actions speak louder than words" still rings true. Empty

---

[32] Matthew 7:3-5

apologies—offered just to end a disagreement—can actually cause deeper damage. Over time, "sorry" without change begins to lose its meaning, and your spouse may start to think, *"What's the point? You always say you're sorry, but nothing ever changes."* A real apology brings healing because it's rooted in sincerity and backed by intentional efforts to do better.

When we're quick to own our part—even when it seems small—we send a powerful, beautiful message: *"You are more important to me than my pride or my need to be right."* Ultimately, taking responsibility isn't a burden—it's a blessing. It creates space for growth, healing, deeper trust, and greater intimacy. It's an invitation to become a better partner and to build a marriage grounded in truth, humility, and grace.

Take Responsibility for Your Actions —Application Steps

☑ **Self-Evaluation Exercise**—Before bringing up something your spouse did wrong, take a moment to ask yourself, "What part of this situation might I have contributed to?" Start the conversation by owning your piece first, without qualifying it with a reason or excuse.

☑ **Go Beyond the Apology**—Next time you apologise to your spouse for something, add a clear follow-up action step and be sure to follow through on it!

☑ **Name the Barrier**—Identify which barrier—ego, fear, stubbornness, or desire for your own way—tends to trip you up the most. Share it openly with your spouse and invite them to lovingly help you recognise when it's getting in the way.

24

ADOPT A "LIFE-LONG LEARNER" MENTALITY

Remaining Teachable and Growing Together

One of the greatest lessons we've learned in marriage—and in life—is that growth is never ending, rather it's an ongoing adventure. Embracing a life-long learner mindset means understanding that both you and your spouse are constantly evolving— always ready to learn, adapt, and deepen your connection. In our home, we like to joke that the biggest room in the house is the "room for improvement." There's always more to discover, new ways to understand one another, and fresh wisdom to bring into our union.

It can be so easy to fall into the trap of thinking, "I've got this figured out," However, the reality is that marriage is a dynamic, lifelong journey that necessitates constant adaptation and evolution. It demands humility and the courage to admit we don't have all the answers, and the curiosity to seek guidance, whether from mentors, books, or other couples who inspire us.

For us, adopting a growth mindset has made all the difference. It's the simple belief that with dedication, patience, and effort, we can learn and grow and when things go wrong (and trust us, they sometimes do!), having a growth mindset helps us to see setbacks not as failures, but as opportunities to learn and do better. For example, there have been times we made decisions that cost us dearly. It would have been so easy to point fingers or hold grudges, but instead, we chose to step back, learn from what happened, and adjust our approach moving forward. This attitude helped us strengthen our partnership instead of letting mistakes pull us apart. When you know you're both learning, not judging, it creates an environment of support and understanding and enables you to turn challenges into stepping stones, strengthening our bond rather than fraying it.

Studies (Marisa T. Cohen PhD, 2024) show that people with a growth mindset tend to have more satisfying relationships. They're less sensitive to rejection and more open to facing challenges together. And it makes sense — when you see challenges as something to learn from rather than a threat, you're less defensive and more open to the opportunities that often come with the challenge. On the flip side, a fixed mindset can quietly do a lot of damage in a marriage. When you think mistakes define you or your spouse, feedback starts to feel like criticism, and before long, small issues can build walls instead of building trust. When someone makes a mistake and gets harshly criticized instead of receiving compassion, it makes them less willing to be open up next time. Vulnerability starts to feel unsafe, and if that pattern keeps repeating, it can quietly erode the trust and intimacy that relationships so badly need.

Turning Challenges to Opportunities

Every marriage will face its share of challenges— disagreements, misunderstandings, stress, you name it. The real opportunity comes when we start seeing those moments not as dead ends, but as invitations to learn and grow. Maybe you have a communication breakdown — it's a chance to learn better ways to listen and express yourself. Maybe you disagree on parenting styles — that's an opportunity to understand each other's values and work as a team. Maybe one of you makes a risky career decision that doesn't pay off — it can become a moment to learn about resilience and teamwork. Every struggle can become a stepping stone if we're willing to stay teachable and commit to growing and adapting together. You don't have all the answers, neither does your spouse. By embracing a growth mindset, you can navigate challenges with empathy and collaboration, fostering a stronger, more resilient bond.

After decades together, we still find that marriage keeps us humble. It constantly demands that we remain teachable, genuinely willing to listen to each other's perspectives, especially when those perspectives challenge our own deeply held beliefs or assumptions. This requires a conscious effort to truly listen and understand our partner's viewpoint, even if it initially feels uncomfortable or contrary to our own. It is about cultivating a readiness to set aside our preconceived notions and embrace the possibility that our own understanding might be incomplete or even incorrect.

We encourage you to lean into the journey together. Keep asking questions, keep reading, keep inviting fresh ideas into your home. Celebrate every lesson, big and small. When both partners commit to staying curious, open, and teachable, marriage becomes a living, breathing partnership—one that grows stronger, wiser, and more beautiful with each passing day.

Adopt a "Life-Long Learner" Mentality—Application Steps

☑ **Set Growth Goals**—Share with each other one area in which you want to grow over say the next six month. Set a SMART goal to help you achieve your desired growth and hold each other accountable.

☑ **Regularly Share Your Learning**—Each week set aside time to share with each other what you learned that week. It could be something you learnt about yourself as a result of a challenge or a new piece of information or new insight in a particular area.

☑ **Actively Look out for Growth Opportunities**—Next time you face a challenge, rather than giving all your energy to the problem. Deliberately pause, take a step back and ask "what is the growth opportunity here?"

25

AVOID MAKING ASSUMPTIONS

Not Allowing Your Imagination Fill in The Blanks

In the words of Henry Winkler "Assumptions are the termites of relationships." They may seem small and insignificant, but unchecked, they can have massive negative impact on any relationship—just like termites silently destroy the frame of a house from the inside out.

The saying assumption is the lowest level of knowledge is true. When you think about it, assumptions often masquerade as truth, but in reality, they are often just a figment of our imagination. We assume we *know* what our spouse is thinking. We *interpret* their silence, tone, or facial expression based on assumptions. We act on incomplete information, projecting our fears, insecurities, or past experiences onto the present moment. And more often than not, we get it wrong.

It is natural to make assumptions. We do it instinctively, without effort and while assumptions can sometimes be a great starting point, they usually lead to flawed conclusions when unsubstantiated with evidence because when left to fill in the blanks, most people don't default to the best-case scenario. We tend to lean toward the negative. That silence? "They must be angry with me."

 That forgotten message? "They don't care." That sigh? "Here we go again."

What makes assumptions so dangerous is that they often feel like facts. We rarely pause to question them, let alone verify them. Once the assumption is made, we start to find evidence to back it up— after all, no one likes to be wrong. If not careful, even in the face of evidence to the contrary, we stick to our guns and start to act on it—changing our tone, withdrawing affection, holding grudges, or making poor decisions—all without any confirmation that our belief was ever even true!

Assumptions can have long-term negative effects. Assuming your partner knows what you need without telling them could lead to frustration, which in turn could lead to anger and you lashing out, catching them completely off guard because they are completely unaware of how you are feeling. Assuming they are "just being difficult" instead of seeking to understand why they feel the way they do about the issue. Assuming they should "just know" how you feel, instead of communicating your feelings to them. Assuming they are angry with you because they appear aloof and in response withdrawing emotionally, instead of asking if something's wrong. Acting on the basis of assumptions over time erodes intimacy and creates emotional distance. When one constantly feels misunderstood and incorrectly judged, they could begin to withdraw affection and create disconnection to protect themselves.

Assumptions are often based on personal beliefs, biases, and past experiences. They can distort our perception, and the problem with perception is that if unchecked it becomes *our reality,* even if it is not the reality. When Julius and I first met, he admitted he made an assumption: that I probably didn't know how to cook. Apparently, I looked a little too polished, a little *too* classy—definitely more "fine dining" than "home-cooked meals." Now, to his credit, he did say he loved me so much that he was ready to overlook that and survive on takeaways if necessary 😊

We often joke about it, but here's the thing, my assumption was completely wrong. Mary could cook—and very well I might add, thank you very much! Although I do think I am now giving her a run for her money in the cooking department, even if she won't admit it 😊

The point is had that assumption mattered more to me than curiosity, or had I been the kind of guy that just could not imagine himself with a wife that could not cook, that assumption could have prevented me from even initiating a conversation with Mary, let alone pursuing a relationship with her, which would have caused me to miss out on the best thing that's ever happened to me! Do you see how making and acting on assumptions, allowing them to shape our choices could negatively impact our outcomes, causing us to miss out on something—or someone—truly great?

Choose Curiosity Over Assumption

The healthiest relationships are those where both parties stay curious about each other—where they keep learning, keep asking, and never take understanding for granted. Next time you find yourself assuming, pause and instead of immediately acting on it, try these instead.

Ask Questions—Your partner can't read your mind, and you can't read theirs either. Instead of guessing, ask questions to seek clarification. Even when you feel so sure you know what the answer is, ask the questions and give the other party the opportunity to speak for themselves. *"Are you okay?"*, *"Is there something on your mind?"* Ask and listen to what they have to say. You might just find your assumption could not be any further from the truth.

Seek Clarification— Misunderstandings often arise not from what was said, but from what was assumed. Before jumping to conclusions or reacting emotionally, take a moment to ask for clarity. Simple questions like, *"When you said… what did you mean by that?"* can open up honest dialogue and prevent unnecessary conflict. Similarly, instead of assuming your spouse ignored you, try asking, *"Did you hear me when I said…?"* This approach shows maturity, curiosity, and respect. It shifts the dynamic from confrontation to connection. Remember, asking for clarification isn't a sign of stupidity or thickness—it's a sign of wisdom and commitment to understanding each other better.

Communicate Honestly—When your spouse asks questions to understand how you're feeling or clarify a situation, honesty is key. It's not helpful to say "I'm fine" or "everything's okay" when it's obvious that something's wrong. If this becomes a habit, and you only open up after repeated prompting, it sends a confusing message. Over time, your spouse may begin to recognize the patterns in your behaviour and make assumptions based on past experiences, and it would be unfair to blame them.

On the flip side, if you're fully aware of what the issue is but pretend not to, only for it to transpire that you knew all along, it can feel dismissive or even manipulative. Over time, this erodes trust. The next time you genuinely ask, "What's wrong?", they might assume you're just pretending again and choose not to respond. Open, honest communication helps prevent misunderstandings and builds trust.

Don't Make Seeking Clarification Difficult

Depending on your personality style, asking questions—or being open to receiving them—may come naturally to you. For others, however, it can be a source of frustration or irritation. I remember early in our relationship; this was a common point of friction. I would ask Julius questions to clarify something or get more details— whether it was about an idea he had or a family or ministry project—and he would often interpret my questions as a challenge to his idea or a subtle way of expressing disagreement, when in reality, I was simply seeking to understand better.

Reading Mary's DISC Report was a real eye-opener for me. It helped me see that she wasn't being difficult or defiant. Asking questions is just part of how she's wired. She is more detail oriented than I am and so the more informed she is, the better equipped she feels to contribute effectively. Understanding each other's personality and behavioural styles through the Maxwell DISC Personal Profile Report[33] has been a real game changer for our relationship. If you've never explored personality assessment tools, we highly recommend it—they can offer invaluable insights and help you navigate your differences with greater empathy and understanding.

When Assumptions Lead the Way, Connection Gets Lost

---

[33] www. candoacademy.net/discover-your-true-self/

Operating on assumptions is like navigating with a broken compass. You think you're going in the right direction, but you're veering further from your destination. This is especially true in marriage, where emotional intimacy is built not just on shared experiences, but on shared understanding; and understanding only grows when we ask, listen, and communicate openly. Healthy relationships are built on clear communication, not guesswork. So next time you catch yourself thinking "they should know," or "they probably meant...," Pause—Ask. Clarify. Invite dialogue because the only thing more damaging than a wrong assumption... is building your relationship on it.

Make Truth Your Compass

Relying on assumptions in a relationship is like trying to navigate with a faulty compass—you may feel like you're heading in the right direction, but in reality, you could be drifting further from true connection. In marriage, emotional intimacy is nurtured not just by time spent together, but by the depth of mutual understanding, and that understanding only deepens when we take the time to ask, listen, and communicate in with intention.

Thriving relationships are built on clarity and truth, not guesswork. So, the next time you're tempted to think, *"They should know"* or *"They probably meant..."* Pause—Ask the question—Invite the conversation—Seek out Truth. Don't jump to conclusions because few things are more damaging than a wrong assumption—except building your relationship around it.

Avoid making Assumptions—Application Steps

☑ **Keep a check on your emotions**—Next time something feels "off" or your partner says or does something that triggers a reaction, take a breath. Pause before you react. Ask yourself: *"Why am I feeling the way I am feeling?" "Am I jumping to conclusions here or do I know this for sure?"* This short pause can make all the difference between conflict and connection.

☑ **Practice Curious Communication**—Even if you're convinced you know what your spouse meant, choose curiosity over certainty. Try saying, *"This might seem obvious, but I don't want to assume—can you help me understand what you meant?"* It opens the door to understanding their perspective, and you might just discover your assumption was off.

☑ **Have an "Ask Me Anything" Night**—Set aside 20–30 minutes to intentionally connect and clear the air. You each take turns asking the other 2–3 questions you've been curious about, or that might help you understand them better. They can be light-hearted or deeper in nature. For example: "What's something you wish I understood better about you?" *"What's a dream or goal you haven't shared with me* *yet?" ""Have there been moments when you felt misunderstood by me?"* The goal is not necessarily to fix and certainly not to defend—just to listen, clarify, and connect.

26

EMBRACE HUMILITY

Not Taking Yourself Too Seriously

A thriving marriage flourishes in an atmosphere of mutual humility—where neither partner insists on being "right" at the expense of the other or the relationship. Humility is not about thinking less of yourself, it's about thinking of yourself less. Within the context of marriage, it's actively seeking your spouse's wellbeing, and setting aside ego, pride, and self-centeredness. We know this goes against the grain in a world where self is very elevated, and we are all encouraged to put ourselves first. Don't get us wrong, self-care and self-love is important. If we are not ok, we won't be of much good to anyone. However, you cannot expect to always look out first for yourself, always putting your needs, your opinions, your desires first, and expect the relationship to thrive. Nobody wants to be play second fiddle all the time.

Left unchecked, barriers such as stubbornness, selfishness, fear of rejection and fear of being taken advantage of can erode trust, erect guards, leaving both parties feeling isolated. By contrast, embracing humility builds bridges of understanding and fosters emotional safety.

Why Embracing Humility Matters

Like we stated in an earlier chapter, marriage is not a contest— it's a partnership grounded in love, respect, and shared purpose. When humility is present:

Trust Deepens: When you see your spouse freely acknowledge their own mistakes—without defensiveness or elaborate excuses—it signals a commitment to honesty and transparency. Over time, these open admissions break down walls of suspicion and instead of wondering what else they might be hiding, you come to expect that errors will be owned quickly, lessons will be learned, and past mis-steps won't be swept under the rug. You know your partner is reliable because they will tell you the truth, even when it's uncomfortable. In our marriage, we've found that when one of us admits fault, it immediately diffuses tension and allows us to move forward together, rather than retreat into doubt. That willingness to be vulnerable and accountable invites us both to extend grace, deepens our sense of safety, and cements the trust that forms the bedrock of our relationship.

Conflict Resolution Improves: Few phrases have the power to deescalate tension and open the door to healing like a sincere "I'm sorry." Yet, pride and stubbornness often hold us back from uttering these words, causing conflicts to linger and wounds to deepen. In our marriage, Julius has always been quick to apologise—sometimes, perhaps, too quick. As we've discussed earlier, offering an apology merely to restore peace, without accompanying it with meaningful change, can render the words hollow over time. I on the other hand, found it more challenging to apologise. After an argument and his apology, Julius would often ask, "Aren't you going to say sorry too?" My typical retort was, "what for? I didn't do anything wrong." Few things embody ego more than the belief that you are always right. Acknowledging our own faults and extending genuine apologies require humility and self-awareness. It's not necessarily about conceding defeat but about valuing the relationship over the need to be right. By embracing this mindset, we've learned that sincere apologies, coupled with efforts to change, strengthen our bond and foster a more resilient partnership.

Emotional Intimacy Grows. Embracing humility creates a safe emotional climate where both parties can be truly vulnerable—an essential foundation for deep intimacy. When you consciously set aside your own agenda and open up to your partner's views and seek to understand them rather than simply insisting on your own way, you're sending the message that your spouse matters, and this will only strengthen your emotional bond.

Common Barriers to Humility

Even the most well-intentioned couples can stumble over:

Ego and Pride: The urge to be right, to feel superior, or to be in control can block apology and empathy. Our inherent human tendency towards pride will undoubtedly be a significant hurdle. Ego will make it difficult to admit mistakes, apologise sincerely, or value our spouse's perspective equally.

Selfishness: When personal comfort or convenience trumps your spouse's needs, it undercuts the very selfless love you committed to with your vows When we prioritise our own needs, desires, and comfort above our spouse's, it leaves little room for the selfless nature of humility. A "me-first" attitude clashes directly with putting the other person first.

Insecurity: Paradoxically, insecurity—a feeling of inadequacy and having doubts about one's own worth—may drive defensiveness tempting you to guard against imagined failures rather than allowing yourself to be vulnerable. You could end up creating a need to always be right just to prove your worth, rather than allowing yourself to be vulnerable enough to admit shortcomings so you can both move on.

Stubbornness and Power Struggles: A refusal to budge even on minor issues signals "my way or no way," straining cooperation and mutual respect. Power dynamics can be subtle or overt in any relationship. A desire to "win" or be dominant can directly oppose the give-and-take and mutual submission inherent in humility.

Unrealistic Expectations: Holding onto rigid or unrealistic expectations of our spouse can hinder humility. Rather than approaching them with understanding and grace, we might become critical and judgmental when they don't meet our standards.

Cultivating Humility in Your Marriage

Lead with "We," Not "Me." Not necessarily verbally, but in your thinking and approach, focus on unity and how you can handle the situation so you both feel heard. It's not me against you; it's us against whatever the situation is. Begin difficult conversations by affirming your shared goal, which is that you find a solution together. These practical steps encourage a shift away from self-centeredness towards a mindset that prioritises and values your spouse.

We can't say we've perfected this in our marriage, but we rest in the certainty of one another's selfless love. We trust that every suggestion and decision springs from genuine care—for each other, for our relationship, and for our home—so we feel secure knowing no choice is rooted in selfishness. Even when we disagree, one of us can simply say, "alright, go ahead," confident that the other's intentions are pure. In our union, one partner's joy truly becomes the other's.

Humility may not come naturally to everyone, and it can be more difficult for some than others, but it can certainly be cultivated.

First, recognise that this is not a competition or a tug-of-war; this is marriage! You are building a life together and are in this for the long haul. You are here to support, serve, and protect each other—make this your daily goal. Remember, embracing humility isn't a sign of weakness—it's the pathway to deeper connection, healing, and a marriage that reflects the grace you both long to give and receive.

Embrace Humility—Application Steps

☑ **Look out For Opportunities to Serve** —Regularly seek out small ways to serve your spouse and make their life easier. This could be taking on a task they dislike, offering help without being asked, or simply anticipating their needs.

☑ **Watch Your Attitude to Correction**—How do you respond to correction, either from your spouse or others. If you are quick to get defensive or make excuses, check your heart, pride might just be lurking there.

☑ **Praise Instead of Comparison**—If your first instinct is to measure your partner's efforts against your own or point out what they could've done better, pause and reverse that reflex. Lead with a heartfelt compliment—highlight something they did well and express genuine appreciation. Over time, your focus on praising rather than comparing or criticising will cultivate an atmosphere of encouragement and mutual respect.

27

LEVERAGE THE POWER OF AGREEMENT

Prioritizing Unity Above All

In Marriage, we are undoubtedly stronger together, and our efforts yield better results when we operate as one. It's no wonder the Bible says, "Two people are better than one, because they get more done by working together."[34] There is nowhere this holds truer than in marriage. Unity is critical to the survival and well-being of our relationship; disunity will derail our purpose, lead to chaos, cause a great deal of heartache, and may even lead to divorce if care is not taken. To safeguard against these dangers, we must be vigilant and look out for anything that could sow seeds of disunity in our marriage.

Our unity is one of our non-negotiables. From the onset of our relationship, we recognised that if we were going to build a strong marriage that would stand the test of time, we needed

---

[34] Ecclesiastes 4:9

to build together, so we cherish and protect our union, not allowing any internal or external factors to come between us. Thankfully, it didn't require us to convince the other; we both knew it had to be done at all costs. We would rather give up our *"right"* than break that bond of peace and unity in our home. It really is our superpower. We know that if we stand together, there is nothing we cannot overcome. However, if we are divided, we are defeated already because a house divided against itself cannot stand.[35]

For us, unity isn't merely about keeping the peace or being on the same page—it's a spiritual reality rooted in our Christian faith. When we join hands in prayer, speaking with one voice and unwavering faith we release God's supernatural power into our circumstances. As Jesus promised, "If two of you agree about anything on earth, it will be done for you by my Father in heaven."[36] We'll explore the power of prayer in a later chapter, but for now, remember: nothing is more vital than protecting your unity, because that is where your greatest strength lies.

There are several factors that could lead to disunity; some are obvious, and some, perhaps less so. Let's explore some of them.

---

[35] Matthew 12:25
[36] Matthew 18:19

Lack of Shared Goals and Vision: Two can't walk together unless they agree.[37] We addressed the importance of having shared goals in an earlier chapter. We encourage you to read that together as a couple and put it into practice, because differing visions will inevitably lead to division.

Unresolved Issues: Disagreements and conflicts are a natural part of any relationship but must not be allowed to fester. If they do, we begin to lose trust and disconnect emotionally, which can seriously undermine our unity. It is also possible that one or both of you have had previous relationships that did not go so well, and you may have developed some safeguarding mechanisms that could prevent you from opening up in your new relationship. It's essential to address these wounds head-on and, when needed, seek professional support to heal. Otherwise, unhealed pain from the past may block the joy and intimacy you deserve in your current partnership.

Lack of Intimacy: Intimacy, encompassing emotional closeness and physical connection, is vital to a strong marriage. When it wanes or becomes unbalanced, it can lead to feelings of loneliness, rejection, and weakening of our marital bond.

Differing Priorities: Individuals may have different priorities in life, whether related to career, family, social life, or personal interests. When these priorities clash and we don't find ways

---

[37] Amos 3:3

to compromise and support each other's needs, we can feel pulled in different directions and create a sense of disunity.

Financial Disagreements: Money is a practical aspect of life that can become a significant source of tension if we have different spending habits, saving goals, or views on financial management and don>t find a way to work together as a team. Talk through these issues, get a coach to help align your financial goals if necessary.

Unmet Expectations: We often enter marriage with certain expectations, sometimes unspoken, about what our roles and responsibilities, and that of our spouse should be. They say disappointment is the gap between expectation and reality, and this is true. Unmet expectations could leave one party feeling like they got the raw end of the deal and this could cause discord. This takes us back to the very first chapter of this book, and the importance of communicating your expectations, even before you say "I Do." Communicating expectations upfront minimises disappointments later.

Poor Communication: Too often we speak without truly listening—failing to seek first to understand before asking to be understood—or we pretend problems don't exist, resorting to the silent treatment instead of dialogue. This breakdown breeds discord. Couples can spend hours arguing only to discover they were really saying the same thing all along. Imagine how much stress and tension could have been avoided if they had simply listened to each other. Investing in enhancing your communication skills is one of the most valuable gifts you can give your marriage, saving you both unnecessary stress and heartache. Read a book, take a course, get coaching—you and your relationship are well worth it!

External Stressors: Life is full of challenges and most are unexpected—job loss, serious illness, family crises, or the heartbreak of miscarriage. Even the strongest bonds can feel strained under such weight. The key is facing these pressures as a united front. For us, that means speaking honestly about our pain, fears and frustrations—no holding back. When one of us falters under the strain, the other steps in to offer strength and encouragement. And sometimes, words fail us entirely; in those moments, we simply sit together in silence, wrapped in each other's arms. Whatever the case, we weather it side by side.

Outside Influences: It is not uncommon for friends or even parents to pass on their ingrained fears or biases. Statements like "You have to be very careful with men" or "Women cannot be trusted" often stem from their personal experiences or the experiences of someone they love and respect. They may share these beliefs to ensure you don't suffer the same pain they did. We recall one of Julius' friends advising him to buy all the clothes he wanted now because after he gets married, he won't have the luxury, as his wife will spend all his money. It was said jokingly, but with an underlying seriousness. The mouth always speaks what's in the heart, even if said jokingly.[38] Just imagine Julius taking this advice and securing what he needed thirty years ago—how beneficial would that be now? ☺

Entering a relationship with complete openness and vulnerability is inherently risky, as we hope the other person will reciprocate. But the truth is, we cannot create absolute unity any other way. Over the last thirty years, we have learned to just trust each other; we are completely vulnerable with each other, simply because we have come to accept that we both have each other's best interests at heart. As a result, it has not been a struggle for us to open up to one another. You might argue that your spouse is different, and we would agree. However, consider this: if you are holding back, it might be the reason your spouse isn't opening up either. In life, we often receive what we give.

Ultimately, the strength and resilience of our marriage are intrinsically linked to the unity we cultivate. By consciously prioritising agreement and zero tolerance to strife, actively nurturing our bond, we build a foundation that can withstand the inevitable storms of life and allows us to truly thrive together, hand in hand, wherever our journey takes us.

---

[38] Matthew 12:34

Leverage The Power of Agreement—Application Steps

☑ **Prioritise Shared Goals**—Discuss and define your shared goals and vision for your marriage and family and make decisions together. Regularly revisit these to ensure you are both working towards the same objectives.

☑ **Address Issues Promptly**—Don't let disagreements or conflicts linger and fester. Develop healthy communication strategies to address issues as they arise, working towards understanding and resolution to prevent emotional disconnection.

☑ **Communicate Expectations Openly**—Have honest conversations about your expectations in the marriage regarding roles, responsibilities, and how you envision your life together. This helps to avoid misunderstandings and unmet needs that can lead to disunity.

28

MAKE GOD THE CENTRE OF YOUR MARRIAGE

Building a Re-enforced Cord That Cannot Be Broken

Throughout this book, we've aimed to be as open and transparent as possible, sharing both our successes and our shortcomings. It would be incomplete—if not outright dishonest—for us to end without talking about what we believe is the true "secret sauce" behind our lasting marriage. In this chapter and the next, we want to let you in on what has made the most profound difference for us. Now, depending on your beliefs, it might seem unusual to include a chapter about God in a book on how to divorce-proof your marriage, but we ask you to stay with us. You've come this far—why not come all the way? 😊 Whether you're a person of strong faith, curious faith, or no faith, we believe you'll find encouragement in what we're about to share. You might even be surprised by just how relevant it is to your journey.

For us, God isn't just an important part of our lives—He's the very centre. His presence influences everything: how we think, how we act, the choices we make, and how we live day to day. In a world that constantly shifts and where "truth" seems to evolve with opinion and emotion, we've chosen to build our lives—and our marriage—on a truth that never changes. God is our constant, our firm foundation, our unshakable rock. We find deep comfort in knowing He is reliable and never fails. And truthfully, we're 100% certain that we wouldn't have made it through three decades of marriage without His presence, His guidance, and His grace. He is our core, our fortress, our unfailing strength, and our ever-present help in time of need.[39]

Scripture gives a powerful illustration of the power of unity. It tells us that one person alone can be overpowered, but two can stand back-to-back and conquer. Then it paints an even stronger image: "a cord of three strands is not easily broken."[40] Marriage is undoubtedly strong when built on love and commitment. But when God becomes that third strand—woven into every fibre of your relationship—it transforms your union into a spiritual covenant, infused with divine strength and wisdom. It's no longer just about sharing a life—it becomes a journey of faith, where God's word serves as the compass guiding you through every season.

---

[39] Psalm 46:1
[40] Ecclesiastes 4:12

The Foundation of Marriage

We truly believe that God is the architect of marriage. He designed it, and no one understands how it works better than the One who created it. When He becomes the solid foundation of your home and the heartbeat of your relationship, He becomes the one who holds it all together. His word—the ultimate blueprint for marriage— offers wisdom on how to love unconditionally, respect and honour wholeheartedly, forgive freely, and sacrifice willingly. It teaches us that marriage is far more than a legal contract; it is a sacred covenant, divinely ordained and eternally significant.

The Power of God's Word—Our Shared Truth

Two people cannot each hold tightly to opposing beliefs and both claim to have the "truth." Eventually, one must ask: what is the truth we both submit to? If truth becomes subjective— based solely on feelings or shifting emotions—then unity becomes nearly impossible. Marriage brings together two individuals from different upbringings, cultures, and worldviews. So how do you build something truly unified? For us, the answer has been our mutual submission to God's word. It's the constant we both return to when our perspectives clash or emotions run high. It's the referee we've agreed on, the unchanging authority we trust to help us bridge our differences.

This isn't just a nice idea to us. God's word isn't a dusty book of old rules and rituals—it is alive. It speaks, it leads, it comforts, it convicts. When we allow it to shape our thinking and decisions, we find ourselves grounded even in the most turbulent times. God's word anchors our marriage in storms, offers us refuge when we're weary, and empowers us when we feel weak. Within its pages, we find not only truth, but healing, direction, peace, and clarity.

This shared foundation doesn't eliminate all disagreements, but it changes how we approach them. When you're both committed to submitting to a higher truth and allowing God's Spirit to work in your hearts, it becomes easier to let go of pride, listen with compassion, and forgive with sincerity.

Marriage without God can certainly work, but for us, it would be like sailing a ship without a compass. With Him at the centre, we're not only surviving the storms—we're learning to thrive through them, together.

We'd love to share some of the practical ways the Bible has shaped and guided our marriage over the years.

Loving as God Loves

At the heart of the Bible is love—pure, selfless, unconditional love. Scripture doesn't just describe God as loving; it defines Him as Love itself. His love for us is passionate, unwavering, and never-ending. The Bible calls us to reflect that same kind of love in our relationships[41]—to use it as the standard we strive toward. God's love sets the bar: it is sacrificial, patient, and deeply committed. We'll be the first to admit we don't always hit that mark; we're human, after all, and sometimes we fall short. But we've also seen the painful consequences of choosing anything less than love. That's why we make a conscious effort, again and again, to choose love—especially when it's hardest to do so.

Respect and Honour

One of the core teachings of Scripture about marriage is the importance of mutual respect and honour. The Bible gently yet powerfully reminds us to listen to one another with intention, to value each other's perspectives, and to treat each other with respect and honour. God wants us to honour each other. The husband should honour his wife,[42] and the wife should honour her husband.[43] None is superior to the other, contrary to some cultural beliefs and practices. Respect isn't just about polite words or surface gestures—it's about seeing your spouse as God sees them: worthy of love, attention, and honour. When respect is present, love deepens. When it's missing, even the strongest relationships can suffer.

---

[41] John 13:34
[42] 1st Peter 3:7
[43] Ephesians 5:21

Forgiveness and Reconciliation

Forgiveness is not optional in marriage—it's essential. Conflict is inevitable when two imperfect people live closely together, but how we handle it makes all the difference. The Bible teaches us to forgive as we have been forgiven—freely, completely, and from the heart.[44] Holding onto resentment only leads to emotional distance, but forgiveness paves the way for healing and connection. It's not always easy, but it's always worth it. We've learned to prioritise reconciliation, creating space for honest conversations, emotional release, and fresh starts.

Sacrifice and Service

The Bible consistently calls us to serve one another in love, just as Christ served and sacrificed for us.[45] In marriage, this means putting your spouse's needs ahead of your own—not because you're keeping score, but because love naturally leans toward giving. Serving each other builds trust, softens hearts, and keeps pride at bay. We've found that the more we look for small, practical ways to serve one another, the more connected and secure we feel in our relationship.

---

[44] Ephesians 4:32
[45] Galatians 5:13

Navigating Financial Strain

The Bible may not read like a financial textbook, but it's full of practical wisdom about money: from managing resources and avoiding debt, to living generously and stewarding wisely. We've discovered firsthand how applying these principles has brought clarity and stability to our finances. Searching Scripture together and seeking God's guidance has helped us make wise decisions and avoid unnecessary stress in this area.

Parenting Differences

People often say children don't come with instruction manuals—but we've found the Bible to be just that: a timeless and trustworthy guide for parenting. From teaching discipline and love to modelling character and faith, Scripture offers profound insight into raising children with purpose and intention. When we face differences in our parenting styles, we turn to the Bible for guidance, and it has consistently helped us to navigate parenthood with wisdom and grace.

The Enduring Legacy of a God-Centred Marriage

By consciously and consistently placing God at the centre of our marriage, we are not just building a life together for ourselves; we are establishing a legacy of faith and love that will hopefully last for generations. We are laying a solid and unshakeable foundation of love, unity, and spiritual strength that will not only support us through life's inevitable challenges and steadfastly guide us toward an even brighter future but will also act as a guiding light for our children and the generations after them.

Life is a mix of mountaintop highs and valley lows—and marriage experiences both. When trials come, as they inevitably do, the strength of your foundation becomes clear. We've learned that facing challenges together, with God at the centre, gives us confidence that we'll come out stronger on the other side. With Him walking beside us, we've never had to face a storm alone.

Make God the Centre of Your Marriage— Application Steps

☑ **Study God's Word Together**—Set time apart every week to study God's word together. If you have children, get the children involved. Read a passage of scripture and have everyone share something they learned or an insight they gained.

☑ **Pray Together Every day**—Invite God into your daily lives in prayer. It need not be a 30 minute or hour-long prayer, but endeavour to pray together every day and pray about everything. We never bother God when we pray. Whatever challenges you are facing in your relationship— big or small, bring it to the Lord in prayer.

☑ **Attending the Same Place of Worship**—The idea of a husband and wife attending different places of worship is not a great one. It's important that you expose yourselves to the same spiritual atmosphere.

29

MAKE PRAYER YOUR FIRST RESPONSE

Tapping into Heaven's Power and Provision

We would now like to share with you another aspect of our "secret sauce"—prayer. We believe that God's care extends to the most minute aspects of our lives, both as individuals and as a couple. Prayer is a direct line of communication to the One who holds all things together. We are deeply grateful for a God who is both intimately involved in our personal journeys and readily accessible to us as a couple. Looking back, we can both testify to the countless occasions where we have witnessed God's intervention, His guidance, and His provision in ways that have strengthened our faith and our marriage immeasurably.

Just as a shared vision acts as a vital roadmap, charting the course for our family's journey through life, so too does praying together. Prayer is more than just a religious duty; it is a powerful tool for deepening our connection with each other and with God. It serves as a wellspring of inner strength, offering solace in times of difficulty and amplifying our joys in moments of celebration. Through prayer, we intentionally invite God's presence, His peace, and His divine perspective into the very fabric of our family life, allowing Him to shape and guide us.

While we approach this topic with sensitivity, we also feel it is important to acknowledge that there are spiritual forces at play in this world that actively seek to undermine the sanctity and success of marriage. These are not battles fought with earthly weapons, but rather through spiritual means. Therefore, engaging in prayer together becomes an essential form of spiritual warfare, a powerful way to stand firm against negativity and protect the sacred bond we share.

The power of collective prayer, when two hearts and minds unite in seeking God's will, transcends simply reciting memorised words or passively reading someone else's prayer. While these can sometimes be helpful or even therapeutic, true prayer for us is a deeply personal and authentic conversation, a genuine engagement with God expressed in our own everyday language. We believe in cutting through religious jargon and simply speaking freely and honestly with Him, just as we would confide in a close and trusted friend because that is precisely the intimate relationship, He desires to have with each of us. And when we, as a couple, come together, setting aside our individual concerns and uniting our hearts to present our requests and praises before God, we believe we unleash a uniquely effective and unstoppable power, a synergy that amplifies our faith and invites His transformative work into our lives.

We've lost count of how many times we've found ourselves at our wits end—confused, overwhelmed, and unsure of what to do next. In those moments, we've turned to God in prayer, and time and again, we've seen Him move in powerful, sometimes unexpected ways. Whether through miraculous provision, divine wisdom, or the quiet strength and peace to endure, God has always met us where we are. From parenting challenges— and some of our children have been more challenging than others—to health issues, financial strain, or needing direction, we've consistently brought it all before the Lord in prayer. And through it all, He has remained faithful.

There have also been deeply painful seasons in our relationship when it felt like we had reached the end of the road. We talked, and talked, and talked—trying everything we knew to resolve the issues—only to feel more stuck and frustrated. It began to feel hopeless, like we were going in circles. At one point, we even wondered if we were just delaying the inevitable. But despite how things looked, our faith wouldn't let us give up. We held onto one unshakable truth: "With God, all things are possible.''[46] His Word tells us that He hates divorce.[47] Not because He wants us to suffer, but because He desires for marriages to thrive. That gave us hope, because we wanted our marriage to succeed too. We just didn't know how.

But here's what we've learned: not knowing the answer doesn't mean there isn't one. Just because we can't see a way out doesn't mean there isn't a way. So, in those moments of despair—when conversations fail, when solutions are nowhere in sight, when we do not know what to do—we do the one thing we know to do: we hold hands and pray. We give it all to God, trusting that He sees what we can't and knows what we don't. Without fail, He shows us the way. Because He always knows the way—He is The Way.

If you're a person of faith, let us encourage you—don't treat prayer as your last resort. Make it your first response. There's an old hymn that says it beautifully:

"Oh what peace we often forfeit, Oh what needless pain we bear,

All because we do not carry Everything to God in prayer."

If you're not someone who prays or considers yourself religious, we still encourage you to give prayer a try. You weren't meant to carry your burdens alone. The Apostle Peter offers this timeless wisdom *"cast all your anxiety on him because he*

---

[46] Matthew 19:26
[47] Malachi 2:16

cares for you.[48] And He truly does. God cares deeply about your marriage—more than you may even realise. Invite Him into your journey. You may be surprised by how He steps in, bringing hope where there was despair, beauty from brokenness, and life to what felt truly dead and buried.

Make Prayer Your First Response—Application Steps

☑ **Daily Moments of Gratitude**—Make gratitude your default response to everything, even the challenging moments. Gratitude immediately shifts your energy from negativity to positivity. Don't do it religiously, but in faith knowing it will all work out in the end because God causes all things to work for the good of those who love Him and are called according to His purpose.[49]

☑ **Weave Prayer Time into Everyday Activities**—Look for simple, natural opportunities to pray together—like before meals or at bedtime. Chances are, you eat at least once a day and go to bed every night (we certainly hope so! 😊). Even if the day feels packed or chaotic, you'll know there's always at least one moment to come together in prayer.

---

[48] 1st Peter 5:7
[49] Romans 8:28

☑ **Create Time and Space**—Choose a specific time and space in your home dedicated to prayer—whether it's beside your bed or on the living room sofa, early in the morning, or just before bed. Establishing a consistent time and location helps you approach prayer as an important appointment with God, reinforcing the habit of praying every day.

30

BE PATIENT WITH EACH OTHER

Rome Was Not Built in a Day

Building a life together with someone else is no small feat. Marriage isn't a sprint; it's a marathon—one that demands endurance, resilience, and above all, patience. You might think, *"Yes, I'll need a lot of patience with my spouse,"* and that's certainly true. But just as vital is the patience you extend to yourself along the way. In the beautiful, often complex dance of marriage—where two unique individuals strive to move as one—patience becomes the quiet rhythm that steadies the inevitable stumbles. It's the gentle understanding that real growth and change takes time.

Patience in marriage is not simply about waiting for your spouse to change. It also means allowing them to patiently walk alongside you as you grow. It's a mutual grace—offering empathy during moments of frustration and trusting in the continual growth happening within each of you. We're all works in progress, navigating our personal journeys while co-creating a shared one. Just like a seedling in a garden, a relationship needs gentle, consistent care to take root and flourish. Patience nurtures that growth—it resists the urge to rush, to demand instant perfection, or to be discouraged by the flaws that naturally surface.

Remember, you and your spouse are two different people with distinct backgrounds, perspectives, and expectations. Those differences are normal. When handled with care, they can become sources of richness in your relationship, highlighting complementary strengths. But without patience, those same differences can lead to friction and division. Patience gives us the capacity to listen deeply, understand the other's perspective, and find common ground instead of letting our differences pull us apart.

Over time, we all evolve. Interests change, priorities shift, and our understanding of ourselves and the world matures. Patience helps us embrace these changes in each other and offer steady support through every season of transformation. On the flip side, a lack of patience can quietly erode the foundations of your marriage. It shows up as irritability, quick tempers, and premature assumptions. It can create tension, leaving your partner feeling judged, inadequate, and emotionally unsafe. Impatience chokes communication, breeds resentment, and blocks the very growth and connection we long for.

The truth is, patience doesn't come naturally to most of us—it's something we grow into, and that growth takes time and intentional effort. It starts with self-awareness: identifying your triggers and asking yourself, *"Why was I so impatient?"* and *"How can I respond differently next time?"* Cultivating patience means doing the internal work. It means developing better listening skills, becoming more empathetic, and choosing to respond with grace even when frustration comes knocking.

Patience is also one of the most powerful tools in conflict resolution. Disagreements are inevitable in any intimate relationship, but when you bring patience into the conversation, you create space for real understanding and healing. You approach conflict with a long-term perspective, choosing peace over pride and connection over control. Patience empowers you to trust in the resilience of your relationship and in each other's commitment to make it through.

Here's the truth: strong, lasting relationships aren't built overnight. They're built over time—through daily acts of kindness, consistent support, and a shared commitment to grow. You won't get it right every time, and that's okay. What matters most is that you keep showing up with love, humility, and a heart willing to try again. So be patient. With your spouse. With the process. With yourself. Because just like Rome, a beautiful marriage isn't built in a day—but brick by brick, with time, grace, and patience, you'll build something truly enduring and extraordinary.

Be Patient With Each Other—Application Steps

☑ **Be Slow to Speak**—Before reacting or responding to something your partner says that triggers you, take a deliberate pause (even a few seconds) to truly process their words and your initial reaction. This creates space for a more thoughtful response.

☑ **Empathy Check-In**—Try to see things from your partner's perspective. Briefly ask yourself, "Why might they be feeling or acting this way?" This fosters understanding and reduces impatience.

☑ **Focus on Long-Term**—In moments of frustration, gently remind yourself of your shared long-term goal. Remember you are on the same team trying to build not tear down. So don't respond or make decisions based purely on where you are right now but make decisions based on where you want to go.

OUR PRAYER FOR YOU

Our prayer is that your marriage will be blessed beyond measure, and that you will live in peace and harmony as you allow God to guide and lead you. We also pray that if there is any pain or hurt, that God will bring healing to those areas, and if forgiveness is needed, He will give you the grace to let go, so that you may both blossom and enjoy a long, happy and fulfilling union.

God bless you, your marriage and your family.

Julius and Mary Eniolu

LET'S KEEP IN TOUCH

Keep in touch with Julius and Mary Eniolu by following them on YouTube, Facebook, Instagram and TikTok @ RelationshipRealTalk_JnM.

Julius and Mary are available for talks, keynotes, panel discussions or chat shows. To book them to speak at your next event and for general enquiries please email: hello@eternalharmonyretreats.com or send a message via any of their social media platforms.

NOTES